3B

FOUR CORNERS

Second Edition

Student's Book
with Digital Pack

JACK C. RICHARDS & DAVID BOHLKE

Shaftesbury Road, Cambridge CB2 8EA, United Kingdom

One Liberty Plaza, 20th Floor, New York, NY 10006, USA

477 Williamstown Road, Port Melbourne, VIC 3207, Australia

314–321, 3rd Floor, Plot 3, Splendor Forum, Jasola District Centre, New Delhi – 110025, India

103 Penang Road, #05–06/07, Visioncrest Commercial, Singapore 238467

Cambridge University Press & Assessment is a department of the University of Cambridge.

We share the University's mission to contribute to society through the pursuit of education, learning and research at the highest international levels of excellence.

www.cambridge.org
Information on this title: www.cambridge.org/9781009286558

First published 2012
Second edition 2019

20 19 18 17 16 15 14 13 12 11 10

Printed in Dubai by Oriental Press

A catalogue record for this publication is available from the British Library

ISBN 978-1-009-28653-4   Student's Book with Digital Pack 3
ISBN 978-1-009-28654-1   Student's Book with Digital Pack 3A
ISBN 978-1-009-28655-8   Student's Book with Digital Pack 3B
ISBN 978-1-108-55995-9   Teacher's Edition with Complete Assessment Program 3
ISBN 978-1-009-28650-3   Full Contact with Digital Pack 3
ISBN 978-1-009-28651-0   Full Contact with Digital Pack 3A
ISBN 978-1-009-28652-7   Full Contact with Digital Pack 3B
ISBN 978-1-009-28595-7   Presentation Plus Level 3

Additional resources for this publication at www.cambridge.org/fourcorners

Authors' acknowledgments

Many people contributed to the development of *Four Corners*. The authors and publisher would like to particularly thank the following **reviewers**:

Nele Noe, **Academy for Educational Development, Qatar Independent Secondary School for Girls**, Doha, Qatar; Pablo Stucchi, **Antonio Raimondi School** and **Instituto San Ignacio de Loyola**, Lima, Peru; Nadeen Katz, **Asia University**, Tokyo, Japan; Tim Vandenhoek, **Asia University**, Tokyo, Japan; Celso Frade and Sonia Maria Baccari de Godoy, **Associação Alumni**, São Paulo, Brazil; Rosane Bandeira, **Atlanta Idiomas**, Manaus, Brazil; Cacilda Reis da Silva, **Atlanta Idiomas**, Manaus, Brazil; Gretta Sicsu, **Atlanta Idiomas**, Manaus, Brazil; Naila Maria Cañiso Ferreira, **Atlanta Idiomas**, Manaus, Brazil; Hothnã Moraes de Souza Neto, **Atlanta Idiomas**, Manaus, Brazil; Jacqueline Kurtzious, **Atlanta Idiomas**, Manaus, Brazil; José Menezes Ribeiro Neto, **Atlanta Idiomas**, Manaus, Brazil; Sheila Ribeiro Cordeiro, **Atlanta Idiomas**, Manaus, Brazil; Juliana Fernandes, **Atlanta Idiomas**, Manaus, Brazil; Aline Alexandrina da Silva, **Atlanta Idiomas**, Manaus, Brazil; Kari Miller, **Binational Center**, Quito, Ecuador; Alex K. Oliveira, **Boston University**, Boston, MA, USA; Noriko Furuya, **Bunka Gakuen University**, Tokyo, Japan; Robert Hickling, **Bunka Gakuen University**, Tokyo, Japan; John D. Owen, **Bunka Gakuen University**, Tokyo, Japan; Elisabeth Blom, **Casa Thomas Jefferson**, Brasília, Brazil; Lucilena Oliveira Andrade, **Centro Cultural Brasil Estados Unidos (CCBEU Belém)**, Belém, Brazil; Marcelo Franco Borges, **Centro Cultural Brasil Estados Unidos (CCBEU Belém)**, Belém, Brazil; Geysa de Azevedo Moreira, **Centro Cultural Brasil Estados Unidos (CCBEU Belém)**, Belém, Brazil; Anderson Felipe Barbosa Negrão, **Centro Cultural Brasil Estados Unidos (CCBEU Belém)**, Belém, Brazil; Henry Grant, **CCBEU – Campinas**, Campinas, Brazil; Maria do Rosário, **CCBEU – Franca**, Franca, Brazil; Ane Cibele Palma, **CCBEU Inter Americano**, Curitiba, Brazil; Elen Flavia Penques da Costa, **Centro de Cultura Idiomas – Taubaté**, Taubaté, Brazil; Inara Lúcia Castillo Couto, **CEL LEP – São Paulo**, São Paulo, Brazil; Sonia Patricia Cardoso, **Centro de Idiomas Universidad Manuela Beltrán**, Barrio Cedritos, Colombia; Geraldine Itiago Losada, **Centro Universitario Grupo Sol (Musali)**, Mexico City, Mexico; Nick Hilmers, **DePaul University**, Chicago, IL, USA; Monica L. Montemayor Menchaca, **EDIMSA**, Metepec, Mexico; Angela Whitby, **Edu-Idiomas Language School**, Cholula, Puebla, Mexico; Mary Segovia, **El Monte Rosemead Adult School**, Rosemead, CA, USA; Dr. Deborah Aldred, **ELS Language Centers, Middle East Region**, Abu Dhabi, United Arab Emirates; Leslie Lott, **Embassy CES**, Ft. Lauderdale, FL, USA; M. Martha Lengeling, **Escuela de Idiomas**, Guanajuato, Mexico; Pablo Frias, **Escuela de Idiomas UNAPEC**, Santo Domingo, Dominican Republic; Tracy Vanderhoek, **ESL Language Center**, Toronto, Canada; Kris Vicca and Michael McCollister, **Feng Chia University**, Taichung, Taiwan; Flávia Patricia do Nascimento Martins, **First Idiomas**, Sorocaba, Brazil; Andrea Taylor, **Florida State University in Panama**, Panamá, Panama; Carlos Lizárraga González, **Groupo Educativo Angloamericano**, Mexico City, Mexico; Bo-Kyung Lee, **Hankuk University of Foreign Studies**, Seoul, South Korea; Dr. Martin Endley, **Hanyang University**, Seoul, South Korea; Mauro Luiz Pinheiro, **IBEU Ceará**, Ceará, Brazil; Ana Lúcia da Costa Maia de Almeida, **IBEU Copacabana**, Copacabana, Brazil; Maristela Silva, **ICBEU Manaus**, Manaus, Brazil; Magaly Mendes Lemos, **ICBEU São José dos Campos**, São José dos Campos, Brazil; Augusto Pelligrini Filho, **ICBEU São Luis**, São Luis, Brazil; Leonardo Mercado, **ICPNA**, Lima, Peru; Lucia Rangel Lugo, **Instituto Tecnológico de San Luis Potosí**, San Luis Potosí, Mexico; Maria Guadalupe Hernández Lozada, **Instituto Tecnológico de Tlalnepantla**, Tlalnepantla de Baz, Mexico; Karen Stewart, **International House Veracruz**, Veracruz, Mexico; Tom David, **Japan College of Foreign Languages**, Tokyo, Japan; Andy Burki, **Korea University, International Foreign Language School**, Seoul, South Korea; Jinseo Noh, **Kwangwoon University**, Seoul, South Korea; Neil Donachey, **La Salle Junior and Senior High School**, Kagoshima, Japan; Rich Hollingworth, **La Salle Junior and Senior High School**, Kagoshima, Japan; Quentin Kum, **La Salle Junior and Senior High School**, Kagoshima, Japan; Geoff Oliver, **La Salle Junior and Senior High School**, Kagoshima, Japan; Martin Williams, **La Salle Junior and Senior High School**, Kagoshima, Japan; Nadezhda Nazarenko, **Lone Star College**, Houston, TX, USA; Carolyn Ho, **Lone Star College-Cy-Fair**, Cypress, TX, USA; Kaoru Kuwajima, **Meijo University**, Nogoya, Japan; Alice Ya-fen Chou, **National Taiwan University of Science and Technology**, Taipei, Taiwan; Raymond Dreyer, **Northern Essex Community College**, Lawrence, MA, USA; Mary Keter Terzian Megale, **One Way Línguas-Suzano**, São Paulo, Brazil; B. Greg Dunne, **Osaka Shoin Women's University**, Higashi-Osaka, Japan; Robert Maran, **Osaka Shoin Women's University**, Higashi-Osaka, Japan; Bonnie Cheeseman, **Pasadena Community College** and **UCLA American Language Center**, Los Angeles, CA, USA; Simon Banha, **Phil Young's English School**, Curitiba, Brazil; Oh Jun Il, **Pukyong National University**, Busan, South Korea; Carmen Gehrke, **Quatrum English Schools**, Porto Alegre, Brazil; John Duplice, **Rikkyo University**, Tokyo, Japan; Mengjiao Wu, **Shanghai Maritime University**, Shanghai, China; Wilzania da Silva Nascimento, **Senac**, Manaus, Brazil; Miva Silva Kingston, **Senac**, Manaus, Brazil; Lais Lima, **Senac**, Manaus, Brazil; Yuan-hsun Chuang, **Soo Chow University**, Taipei, Taiwan; Wen hsiang Su, **Shih Chien University Kaohsiung Campus**, Kaohsiung, Taiwan; Lynne Kim, **Sun Moon University (Institute for Language Education)**, Cheon An City, Chung Nam, South Korea; Regina Ramalho, **Talken English School**, Curitiba, Brazil; Tatiana Mendonça, **Talken English School**, Curitiba, Brazil; Ricardo Todeschini, **Talken English School**, Curitiba, Brazil; Monica Carvalho da Rocha, **Talken English School**, Joinville, Brazil; Karina Schoene, **Talken English School**, Joinville, Brazil; Diaña Peña Munoz and Zira Kuri, **The Anglo**, Mexico City, Mexico; Christopher Modell, **Tokai University**, Tokyo, Japan; Song-won Kim, **TTI (Teacher's Training Institute)**, Seoul, South Korea; Nancy Alarcón, **UNAM FES Zaragoza Language Center**, Mexico City, Mexico; Laura Emilia Fierro López, **Universidad Autónoma de Baja California**, Mexicali, Mexico; María del Rocío Domínguez Gaona, **Universidad Autónoma de Baja California**, Tijuana, Mexico; Saul Santos Garcia, **Universidad Autónoma de Nayarit**, Nayarit, Mexico; Christian Meléndez, **Universidad Católica de El Salvador**, San Salvador, El Salvador; Irasema Mora Pablo, **Universidad de Guanajuato**, Guanajuato, Mexico; Alberto Peto, **Universidad de Oaxaca**, Tehuantepec, Mexico; Carolina Rodriguez Beltan, **Universidad Manuela Beltrán, Centro Colombo Americano**, and **Universidad Jorge Tadeo Lozano**, Bogotá, Colombia; Nidia Milena Molina Rodriguez, **Universidad Manuela Beltrán** and **Universidad Militar Nueva Granada**, Bogotá, Colombia; Yolima Perez Arias, **Universidad Nacional de Colombia**, Bogotá, Colombia; Héctor Vázquez García, **Universidad Nacional Autónoma de Mexico**, Mexico City, Mexico; Pilar Barrera, **Universidad Técnica de Ambato**, Ambato, Ecuador; Doborah Hulston, **University of Regina**, Regina, Canada; Rebecca J. Shelton, **Valparaiso University, Interlink Language Center**, Valparaiso, IN, USA; Tae Lee, **Yonsei University**, Seodaemun-gu, Seoul, South Korea; Claudia Thereza Nascimento Mendes, **York Language Institute**, Rio de Janeiro, Brazil; Jamila Jenny Hakam, **ELT Consultant**, Muscat, Oman; Stephanie Smith, **ELT Consultant**, Austin, TX, USA.

Scope and sequence

Functional language	Listening and Pronunciation	Reading and Writing	Speaking
Interactions: Giving an opinion Asking for agreement	**Listening:** Common proverbs A personality quiz **Pronunciation:** Reduction of *don't you*	**Reading:** "The Signs of the Zodiac" Descriptions **Writing:** My personality	• Interview about personality traits • *Keep talking*: "Left-brain vs. right-brain" quiz • Discussion about personality assumptions • Information exchange about friends and their personalities • *Keep talking*: Interviews about special people and things • Guessing game to match people and their personality descriptions
Interactions: Giving an approximate answer Avoiding answering	**Listening:** A survey on grocery shopping habits Award winners for environmental work **Pronunciation:** Stress in compound nouns	**Reading:** "One-of-a-Kind Homes" An article **Writing:** A letter about an environmental issue	• Discussion about community environmental problems • *Keep talking*: "Green" quiz • Survey about water usage • Cause and effect • *Keep talking*: Possible outcomes in different situations • Solutions to environmental issues
Interactions: Apologizing Accepting an apology	**Listening:** Apologetic phone calls A radio call-in show **Pronunciation:** Sentence stress	**Reading:** "Addy's Advice" Emails **Writing:** A piece of advice	• Tips for healthy relationships • *Keep talking*: Advice for relationship problems • Role play to apologize and make excuses • Speculations about classmates • *Keep talking*: Speculations about people • Discussion about relationship problems
Interactions: Advising against something Considering advice	**Listening:** Three problems Interviews about accomplishments **Pronunciation:** Stress shifts	**Reading:** "A Walk Across Japan" An interview **Writing:** An accomplishment	• Interview about personal experiences • *Keep talking*: "Find someone who" activity about personal experiences • Role play to give and consider advice • Discussion about hypothetical situations • *Keep talking*: Interview about hypothetical situations • "Find someone who" activity about accomplishments
Interactions: Beginning instructions Continuing instructions Ending instructions	**Listening:** How things work Song dedications **Pronunciation:** Syllable stress	**Reading:** "A Guide to Breaking into the Music Business" A guide **Writing:** A music review	• Guessing game about music • *Keep talking*: Discussion about music • Information exchange with instructions • "Find someone who" activity about recent actions • *Keep talking*: "Find the differences" activity about two friends • Information exchange about songs and memories
Interactions: Asking about preferences Reminding someone of something	**Listening:** Hotel check-in A white-water rafting trip **Pronunciation:** Reduction of verbs	**Reading:** "A Taste of Cairo" A food blog **Writing:** A walking tour	• Interview about vacation activities • *Keep talking*: Comparison of travel preferences • Role play about checking into a hotel • Discussion about extreme sports • *Keep talking*: Plan for a backpacking trip • Information exchange about dream trips

Classroom language

A 🎧 Complete the conversations with the correct sentences. Then listen and check your answers.

> What page are we on?
> Can you repeat that, please?
> What's our homework?
> ✓ Excuse me. I'm very sorry I'm late.
> May I go to the restroom, please?
> Which role do you want to play?

A <u>Excuse me. I'm sorry I'm late.</u>

B That's OK. Next time try to arrive on time.

A _____

B Thirteen. We're doing the Warm-up for Unit 2.

A _____

B Yes. I said, "Please work with a partner."

A _____

B I'll be Student A. You can be Student B.

A _____

B No problem. Please try to be quick.

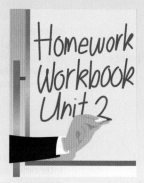

A _____

B Please complete the activities for Unit 2 in your workbook.

B PAIR WORK Practice the conversations.

2

7 Personalities

Lesson A
- Personality traits
- Adverbs modifying adjectives and verbs

Lesson B
- Giving an opinion
- Asking for agreement

Lesson C
- More personality traits
- Present perfect with *for* and *since*

Lesson D
- Reading "The Signs of the Zodiac"
- Writing: My personality

Warm Up

A Describe the people in the picture. Where are they? What are they doing?

B What do you think each person is like? Why?

A You're extremely curious.

1 Vocabulary Personality traits

A 🎧 Match the adjectives and the sentences. Then listen and check your answers.

1 adventurous _____
2 ambitious _____
3 careful _____
4 curious _____
5 easygoing _____
6 optimistic _____
7 outgoing _____
8 stubborn _____

a. I'm interested in learning about people and things around me.
b. I'm friendly, and I like people.
c. I set high goals for myself.
d. I look on the bright side of things.
e. I do things slowly and with attention to detail.
f. I don't like to change my mind.
g. I am relaxed, and I don't worry about little things.
h. I love trying new, exciting activities.

B PAIR WORK Describe people you know with each personality trait. Tell your partner.

"My baby brother is very curious about the world. He wants to touch everything."

2 Language in context Are you a believer?

A 🎧 Read the personality descriptions. Underline the positive personality traits, and circle the negative ones.

Are You Adventurous?

Answer ten questions in this quick personality test to find out just how adventurous you are!

Click here to begin.

Year of the Monkey	Personality Test Results	Your Birth Order
Born in years 1968, 1980, 1992, and 2004 You're extremely curious and outgoing. You solve problems well, but you can be stubborn about some things.	Your score: 13 You're very adventurous, but you're not a very careful person. Try not to make decisions quickly. Take time to consider your options seriously.	As the first-born child in your family, you are a natural leader. You're pretty ambitious and like to work hard. However, you don't work well without direction.

B What about you? Do you believe the things in Part A can tell you about your personality? Why or why not?

3 Grammar 🎧 Adverbs modifying adjectives and verbs

Adverbs that modify adjectives come before the adjectives.	Adverbs that modify verbs go after the verb or the verb and its object.
You're **pretty** ambitious.	You don't work **well** without direction.
You're **extremely** curious and outgoing.	Try not to make decisions **quickly**.

Turn to page 152 for a list of adjective and adverb formations.

A Add the adverbs to the sentences. Then compare with a partner.

1   I move ⌄*slowly* in the morning. (slowly)
2   I'm serious about my studies. (really)
3   I choose my words. (carefully)
4   I arrive at important meetings. (early)
5   My friends are important to me. (extremely)
6   I work in large groups. (well)
7   I'm optimistic about the future. (very)
8   It's easy for me to share my feelings. (fairly)

B PAIR WORK Which sentences in Part A are true for you? Tell your partner.

4 Speaking My true self

A PAIR WORK Interview your partner and ask questions for more information. Take notes.

	Name: _____	Yes	No	Extra information
1	Are you very adventurous?	☐	☐	
2	Do you make new friends easily?	☐	☐	
3	Do you make decisions quickly?	☐	☐	
4	Are you really stubborn about anything?	☐	☐	
5	Do you work and study hard?	☐	☐	
6	Do you get to class early?	☐	☐	
7	Are you completely honest all the time?	☐	☐	

A: Are you very adventurous?

B: Yes, I think so.

A: What's the most adventurous thing you've ever done?

B PAIR WORK Share the most interesting information with another partner.

5 Keep talking!

Go to page 137 for more practice.

I can talk about personality traits. ✓

B In my opinion, . . .

1 Interactions Opinions

A Do you always tell people exactly what you think? Do you sometimes keep your opinions to yourself?

B 🎧 Listen to the conversation. Whose opinion do you agree with more? Then practice the conversation.

Fei Have you seen Adam's new painting?

Ralph Yes. I saw it last weekend.

Fei It's not very good.

Ralph No, it's not. He asked me what I thought of it. I said I didn't think it was his best painting.

Fei You're kidding! How did he react?

Ralph He didn't seem very happy to hear that. But he did ask.

Fei In my opinion, it's better to say something positive, even if you don't really mean it. Don't you agree?

Ralph I don't know. Why do you say that?

Fei Well, it's not always easy to hear the truth.

Ralph I'm not so sure. I find that honesty is always the best policy.

C 🎧 Read the expressions below. Complete each box with a similar expression from the conversation. Then listen and check your answers.

Giving an opinion	Asking for agreement
_____	_____
(If you ask me, . . .)	(Don't you think so?)
(Maybe it's just me, but I think . . .)	(Don't you think that's true?)

D **PAIR WORK** Check (✓) the opinions you agree with. Then ask your partner for agreement.

1 ☐ Women are more stubborn than men.

  ☐ Men are more stubborn than women.

2 ☐ It's never OK to lie.

  ☐ It's sometimes OK to lie.

3 ☐ A small group of friends is better than a large group of friends.

  ☐ A large group of friends is better than a small group of friends.

2 Pronunciation Reduction of *don't you*

A 🎧 **Listen and repeat. Notice how *don't you* is pronounced /dəʊntʃə/.**

Don't you agree?   Don't you think so?   Don't you think that's true?

B **PAIR WORK** **Say the opinions in Exercise 1D again. Ask your partner for agreement. Reduce *don't you* to /dəʊntʃə/.**

3 Listening A book of proverbs

A 🎧 **Listen to Tina and Cal talk about proverbs. Number the proverbs from 1 to 4 in the order you hear them.**

Proverbs	Does Tina agree?	Does Cal agree?
☐ Practice makes perfect.	yes / no	yes / no
☐ Better late than never.	yes / no	yes / no
☐ Beauty is only skin deep.	yes / no	yes / no
☐ Two heads are better than one.	yes / no	yes / no

B 🎧 **Listen again. Do Tina and Cal agree with the proverbs in Part A? Circle *yes* or *no*.**

C **PAIR WORK** **Do you agree with each proverb? Why or why not? Do you know any similar proverbs in your own language? Tell your partner.**

4 Speaking Don't you think so?

A **What's your opinion? Circle the words.**

1 People are **more** / **less** ambitious these days.

2 Young people are **more** / **less** optimistic than older people.

3 **First-born** / **Last-born** children are usually very easygoing.

4 It's **possible** / **impossible** to change your personality.

B **GROUP WORK** **Discuss your opinions from Part A.**

A: *If you ask me, people are less ambitious these days. Don't you think so?*

B: *I'm not so sure. Why do you say that?*

C: *Well, maybe it's just me, but I feel no one wants to work hard these days.*

D: *I'm not sure I really agree. In my opinion, . . .*

C **GROUP WORK** **Think of three other topics. Share your opinions about them. Does anyone agree with you?**

"In my opinion, people worry about their appearance too much. Don't you agree?"

I can give an opinion. ✓
I can ask for agreement. ✓

C We've been friends for six years.

1 Vocabulary More personality traits

A 🎧 **Match the adjectives and the definitions. Then listen and check your answers.**

1	agreeable _____	a.	thinking of the needs of others
2	considerate _____	b.	treating people equally or right
3	decisive _____	c.	friendly and pleasing
4	fair _____	d.	making decisions quickly

5	honest _____	e.	waiting without getting annoyed
6	mature _____	f.	doing what is expected or promised
7	patient _____	g.	truthful
8	reliable _____	h.	behaving in a responsible way

B 🎧 **Complete the chart with the opposites of the words in Part A. Then listen and check your answers.**

dis-	im-	in-	un-
disagreeable			

C **PAIR WORK** **What are the three best personality traits to have in a friend? What are the three worst? Discuss your ideas.**

2 Conversation Time to say you're sorry

A 🎧 **Listen to the conversation. How does Lance describe Jill's reaction?**

Lance   I don't know what to do about my friend Jill. I haven't spoken to her since last weekend, and she won't answer my text messages.

Emily   Did something happen?

Lance   Yeah. I said something about her to another friend. She found out, and now I feel terrible. To be honest, it wasn't anything serious, though. I think she's being unfair and a little immature.

Emily   Well, put yourself in her shoes. Imagine a friend saying something about you behind your back.

Lance   You're probably right.

Emily   Have you been friends for a long time?

Lance   Yes. We've been friends for six years, and we used to talk all the time.

Emily   Then I think you should do the considerate thing and call to say you're sorry.

B 🎧 **Listen to Lance and Jill's phone conversation. What word does Lance use to describe himself?**

3 Grammar 🎧 Present perfect with *for* and *since*

Use the present perfect to describe an action that began in the past and continues to now. Use for *to specify the amount of time. Use* since *to specify the starting point.*

How long have you been friends?
   We've been friends **for six years.**
   We've been friends **since middle school.**
She's been upset **for several days.**
I haven't spoken to her **since last weekend.**

for	since
ten minutes	3:00
two hours	last night
several days	Monday
a month	October
six years	2009
a long time	high school
quite a while	I was a kid

A Complete the sentences with *for* or *since*. Then compare with a partner.

1 Rod has become more considerate _____ he got married.

2 Mr. and Mrs. Kim haven't had an argument _____ 1981.

3 Pete and Lisa have been on the phone _____ six hours.

4 Tim hasn't spoken with his brother _____ a long time.

5 Jay's been totally unreliable _____ he started his new job.

6 Inez has been in her new job _____ three months.

7 Annie has become less immature _____ high school.

8 Jessica and Hector have been married _____ 25 years.

B **PAIR WORK** Ask and answer the questions.

1 How long have you been in this class?

2 What haven't you done since you were a kid?

3 What have you wanted to do for a long time?

4 Speaking Three friends

A Think of three friends. Complete the chart.

	Names	How long we've been friends	Their personality traits
1			
2			
3			

B **GROUP WORK** Tell your group about your friends. Use your information from Part A. Ask and answer questions for more information.

A: I've known my friend Jesse since middle school.

B: What's he like?

A: He's very honest and reliable.

5 Keep talking!

Go to page 138 for more practice.

I can describe people's personalities.

D What is your personality?

1 Reading 🎧

A When were you born? Read the description of your zodiac sign. Does it describe you well?

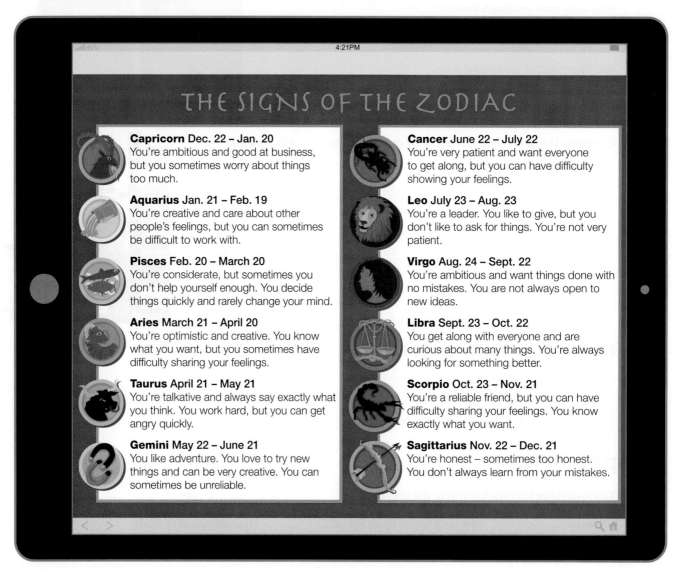

THE SIGNS OF THE ZODIAC

Capricorn Dec. 22 – Jan. 20
You're ambitious and good at business, but you sometimes worry about things too much.

Aquarius Jan. 21 – Feb. 19
You're creative and care about other people's feelings, but you can sometimes be difficult to work with.

Pisces Feb. 20 – March 20
You're considerate, but sometimes you don't help yourself enough. You decide things quickly and rarely change your mind.

Aries March 21 – April 20
You're optimistic and creative. You know what you want, but you sometimes have difficulty sharing your feelings.

Taurus April 21 – May 21
You're talkative and always say exactly what you think. You work hard, but you can get angry quickly.

Gemini May 22 – June 21
You like adventure. You love to try new things and can be very creative. You can sometimes be unreliable.

Cancer June 22 – July 22
You're very patient and want everyone to get along, but you can have difficulty showing your feelings.

Leo July 23 – Aug. 23
You're a leader. You like to give, but you don't like to ask for things. You're not very patient.

Virgo Aug. 24 – Sept. 22
You're ambitious and want things done with no mistakes. You are not always open to new ideas.

Libra Sept. 23 – Oct. 22
You get along with everyone and are curious about many things. You're always looking for something better.

Scorpio Oct. 23 – Nov. 21
You're a reliable friend, but you can have difficulty sharing your feelings. You know exactly what you want.

Sagittarius Nov. 22 – Dec. 21
You're honest – sometimes too honest. You don't always learn from your mistakes.

B Read the chart. Complete the sentences with the correct zodiac signs.

1 A/An _____ hates asking for things.

2 A/An _____ talks a lot.

3 A/An _____ is good at business.

4 A/An _____ wants everything perfect.

5 A/An _____ is adventurous.

6 A/An _____ is decisive.

7 A/An _____ always tells the truth.

8 A/An _____ is difficult to work with.

C **GROUP WORK** Think of three people you know. What is each person's zodiac sign? Does it describe their personalities well? Tell your group.

2 Listening Imagine you're in a forest . . .

A 🎧 **Listen to the personality test. Number the questions from 1 to 7 in the order you hear them.**

☐ What's it made of? _____

☐ Who are you with? _____

☐ What do you do with it? _____

☐ How big is it? _____

☐ What kind do you see? _____

☐ What's on the table? _____

☐ Is it open or closed? _____

B 🎧 **Listen again. Now take the personality test. Answer the questions with your own ideas.**

C PAIR WORK **Compare your answers. Then turn to page 153 to see what your answers mean.**

3 Writing and speaking My personality

A Think about your personality. Answer the questions.

● What are your positive personality traits? _____

● Are there any traits you'd like to change? _____

● Has your personality changed through the years? If so, how? _____

_____

B Write a paragraph about your personality, but do not write your name! Use the model and your answers in Part A to help you.

What am I like?

I'm a pretty easygoing and outgoing person. I'm also very optimistic about the future. I think people like to be around me. However, I can be stubborn sometimes . . .

C GROUP WORK **Put your papers facedown on the table. Take one paper and read the description. Your group guesses who it is and agrees or disagrees with the description. Take turns.**

A: I think that paragraph describes Dana.

B: Yes, that's right. I wrote that one.

C: I agree you're easygoing, Dana, but I don't really think you're stubborn.

B: Yes, I am!

I can talk about my personality. ✓

Wrap-up

1 Quick pair review

Lesson A Test your partner!

Say an adjective. Can your partner write the adverb form correctly? Take turns.
You have two minutes.

"Careful."

1 ____carefully____   3 _____   5 _____

2 _____   4 _____   6 _____

Lesson B Give your opinion!

Look at the two pieces of art. What do you think of them? Give two opinions
about each one. You have two minutes.

A: If you ask me, I think the sculpture is weird. Don't you think so?

B: In my opinion, it's very interesting.

Lesson C Brainstorm!

Make a list of positive and negative personality traits. How many do you know?
You have two minutes.

Lesson D Find out!

Who are two people that you and your partner know with the same personality traits.
You have two minutes.

A: My friend John is really stubborn. Do you know a stubborn person?

B: Yes. My little sister!

2 In the real world

What's your zodiac sign? Find your horoscope from yesterday or last week in an
English-language newspaper, magazine, or website. Was it true? Write about it.

My Horoscope

I'm a Pisces. My horoscope last week said, "You are going to have
a difficult day at work." It was true. I was very busy and nervous
because I had to give a presentation. Luckily, it went very well!

8 The environment

Lesson A
- Environmental impacts
- Quantifiers

Lesson B
- Giving an approximate answer
- Avoiding answering

Lesson C
- Tips to help the environment
- First conditional

Lesson D
- Reading "One-of-a-Kind Homes"
- Writing: Local concerns

Warm Up

A Look at the "before" and "after" pictures. What do you see? What has changed?

B Which was the biggest improvement? Which was the easiest to do? Which was the most difficult?

A Going green

1 Vocabulary Environmental impacts

A 🎧 Label the pictures with the correct words. Then listen and check your answers.

e-waste	hybrid car	organic food	pollution	solar energy
global warming	nuclear energy	plastic bags	recycling bin	wind farm

1 _____

2 _____

3 _____

4 _____

5 _____

6 _____

7 _____

8 _____

9 _____

10 _____

B **PAIR WORK** How do the things in Part A impact the environment?

2 Language in context Green products

A 🎧 Read the ads. What makes each product "green"?

GET GREEN GOODS!

Compact fluorescent lightbulbs
Regular bulbs waste too much energy, so why not use compact fluorescent lightbulbs (CFLs)? They use less energy, and you save more money in the long term.
$20 for a pack of 3

Cloth shopping bag
Who needs paper or plastic? Bring your own cloth bag to the grocery store or mall. This bag makes an important statement and is made of 100% organic cotton.
$5

Recycled toothbrush
Made from 100% recyclable plastic, each toothbrush comes with a reusable travel case. Junior toothbrushes feature endangered animals.
$20 for a pack of 6, or $18 for a pack of 6 Junior toothbrushes

Steel water bottle
Why should we use fewer plastic water bottles? Because too many of them end up in landfills and cause pollution. It's cool to carry your own reusable bottle.
$15

B What about you? Do you own any green products? Would you buy these?

3 Grammar ⌒ Quantifiers

Quantifiers with count nouns	Quantifiers with noncount nouns
We need **more** wind farms.	You can save **more** money with CFLs.
There are**n't enough** recycling bins.	People don't buy **enough** organic food.
There are **too many** bottles in landfills.	Regular lightbulbs use **too much** energy.
People should buy **fewer** plastic bottles.	People should try to use **less** plastic.

A Complete the opinions with quantifiers. Then compare with a partner.

1 "I think it's good that _____ people are buying hybrid cars. They reduce global warming."

2 "In my opinion there's _____ e-waste in our landfills. We need better and safer ways to recycle electronics."

3 "Farmers should grow _____ organic food. I prefer food without chemicals."

4 "Unfortunately, not _____ people use solar power. Is it because it's expensive?"

5 "I feel people should use _____ nuclear energy. Isn't it dangerous?"

6 "Some people say they don't have _____ time to recycle. That's crazy!"

7 "Maybe it's just me, but I think shoppers should take _____ plastic and paper bags from the supermarket. I always bring my own bags."

8 "_____ people throw plastic bottles in garbage cans. They should use recycling bins."

B PAIR WORK Do you agree with the opinions in Part A? Why or why not? Tell your partner.

4 Pronunciation Stress in compound nouns

A ⌒ Listen and repeat. Notice how the first noun in compound nouns often receives stronger stress.

landfill   **light**bulb   **travel** case   **water** bottle

B PAIR WORK Practice the compound nouns. Stress the first noun.

toothbrush   garbage can   recycling bin   wind farm

5 Speaking Our community

A PAIR WORK What environmental problems does your community have? Complete the sentences.

1 There's too much _____ .

2 There isn't enough _____ .

3 We should have fewer _____ .

4 There are too many _____ .

5 There aren't enough _____ .

6 We should use less _____ .

B GROUP WORK Share your ideas with another pair. Did you identify the same problems? Which are the most important?

6 Keep talking!

Go to page 139 for more practice.

I can discuss environmental problems. ⊘

B I'd rather not say.

1 **Interactions** Answering and avoiding answering

A **Imagine these people are asking you questions. Are there any questions they might ask that you think are too personal and that you would not answer?**

| a doctor | a friend | a neighbor | a parent | a stranger | a teacher |

B 🎧 **Listen to the conversation. What question doesn't Jim answer? Then practice the conversation.**

Carl So, Jim, how's the new car?

Jim Hey, Carl. It's great. I'm really happy with it.

Carl It's a hybrid, isn't it?

Jim Yeah. It causes less pollution. I'm trying to do my part to help the environment, you know?

Carl That's great. How long have you had it?

Jim I've only had it for a week.

Carl Really? How many kilometers have you driven?

Jim I'd say about 150.

Carl So, how does it run?

Jim Oh, it runs very well. I'll give you a ride later if you want.

Carl OK, thanks. How much did it cost exactly?

Jim Actually, I'd rather not say. But I know I made a good purchase.

C 🎧 **Read the expressions below. Complete each box with a similar expression from the conversation. Then listen and check your answers.**

Giving an approximate answer	**Avoiding answering**
_____	_____
I'd say maybe . . .	I'd prefer not to say.
Probably . . .	I'd rather not answer that.

D **Match the questions and the responses. Then practice with a partner.**

1 How often do you drive? _____

2 How much do you drive every day? _____

3 How many people have you given rides to? _____

4 How much did you sell your old car for? _____

a. I'd say about ten.

b. Probably five or six times a week.

c. I'd rather not answer that.

d. I'd say about 30 minutes.

2 Listening Consumer research

A 🎧 Listen to a man answer survey questions in a grocery store. Number the questions from 1 to 9 in the order you hear them.

- ☐ Have your buying habits changed in the last year? _____
- ☐1 How often do you walk to the grocery store? *All the time.* _____
- ☐ Do you usually ask for paper or plastic bags? _____
- ☐ How much do you spend on groceries every month? _____
- ☐ How many people are there in your household? _____
- ☐ What is the highest level of education you've completed? _____
- ☐ What do you do for a living? _____
- ☐ Do you ever shop for groceries online? _____
- ☐ How often do you buy environmentally friendly products? _____

B 🎧 Listen again. Write the man's answers.

C **PAIR WORK** Ask and answer the questions in Part A. Answer with your own information, or avoid answering.

3 Speaking Do you waste water?

A Read the survey. Are there any questions you would avoid answering, or is there any information you wouldn't share?

WATER USE SURVEY

Name: _____ Phone number: _____

Address: _____ Email: _____

Age: _____ Education: _____

How many showers do you take in a week? _____

How long do you spend in the shower? _____

Do you ever leave the water running when you brush your teeth? _____

Do you wash dishes by hand or do you use a dishwasher? _____

When you wash dishes, do you leave the water running? _____

When you wash clothes, is the washing machine always completely full? _____

Do you flush the toilet after every use? _____

B **PAIR WORK** Interview your partner. Complete the survey with his or her answers. Mark an ✗ if he or she avoids answering.

C **PAIR WORK** Compare your answers. Who uses more water? How could you use less water?

I can give an approximate answer. ✓
I can avoid answering. ✓

C What will happen?

1 Vocabulary Tips to help the environment

A 🎧 **Match the tips and the pictures. Then listen and check your answers.**

a	Buy local food.	d	Pay bills online.	g	Use cloth shopping bags.
b	Fix leaky faucets.	e	Take public transportation.	h	Use rechargeable batteries.
c	Grow your own food.	f	Use a clothesline.		

 1 ☐
 2 ☐
 3 ☐
 4 ☐

 5 ☐
 6 ☐
 7 ☐
 8 ☐

B **PAIR WORK** **Which things in Part A do you do now? Which don't you do? Tell your partner.**

2 Conversation This is awful!

A 🎧 **Listen to the conversation. When does Kendra want to start taking public transportation?**

Ina   This is awful! It's taking forever to get to work.

Kendra I know. There are just too many cars these days! The traffic seems to get worse and worse.

Ina   Maybe we should start taking public transportation. If we take the subway, we won't have to sit in traffic.

Kendra And we might save money if we take the subway.

Ina   I think you're right. Also, if we take public transportation, we won't get stressed out before work. So, when do we start?

Kendra How about tomorrow?

B 🎧 **Listen to their conversation the next day. What are they unhappy about?**

3 Grammar ∩ First conditional

First conditional sentences describe real possibilities. Use the present tense in the if *clause (the condition).*
Use will *in the main clause.*

If we **take** public transportation, we**'ll save** money.
If we **take** public transportation, we **won't get** stressed out.
Air pollution **will get** worse if we **don't reduce** the number of cars.

Use modals such as may, might, *or* could *in the main clause when you're less certain about the results.*

If air pollution **gets** worse, more people **may get** sick.
If you **don't fix** your leaky faucet, you **might get** a high water bill.
You **could spend** money on other things if you **grow** your own food.

A Write first conditional sentences with the two clauses. Then compare with a partner.

1 you'll use 60 percent less energy / you replace your regular lightbulbs with CFLs
   You'll use 60 percent less energy if you replace your regular lightbulbs with CFLs.

2 you pay your bills online / you'll use less paper

3 we fix our leaky faucets / we'll save water

4 there won't be much air pollution / everyone uses hybrid cars

5 you use a clothesline / other people may start to do the same

6 we use rechargeable batteries / we could save a lot of money

B **PAIR WORK** What else will or may happen for each condition in Part A?
Discuss your ideas.

A: What else will happen if you replace your regular lightbulbs with CFLs?
B: If I replace my regular lightbulbs with CFLs, I'll have cheaper electric bills.

4 Speaking Around the circle

A Write a sentence about what will happen if you change a habit to become greener.

If I grow my own food, I will eat better.

B **GROUP WORK** Sit in a circle. Go around the circle and share your ideas.
Repeat your classmates' main clauses as conditions, and add new ideas.

A: If I grow my own food, I will eat better.
B: If you eat better, you will feel healthier.
C: If you feel healthier, you won't need to go to the doctor very often.

5 Keep talking!

Go to page 140 for more practice.

I can talk about future possibilities. ✓   79

D Finding solutions

1 Reading 🎧

A Look at the pictures. Which home would you prefer to live in? Why?

B Read the article. Write the captions under the correct pictures.

> The Recycled-Tire House   The Found-Object House   The Greenhouse

One-of-a-Kind Homes

Shoichi wanted to live in an environmentally friendly home, and he always liked the greenhouses in his neighborhood in Tokyo, Japan. So he decided to create his own greenhouse-style home. Sunlight warms his new home, and a plastic cover around the house helps to keep the heat inside. There aren't any walls or rooms. The "rooms" are actually large boxes on wheels. He can move them anywhere he likes, even outside. He loves his home, but sometimes he would like to be able to move the whole house.

Ruth is an artist who lives in the Rocky Mountains in the U.S. state of Colorado. Over the years, she found and collected a lot of old objects for her art. When she decided she wanted to live in a more unusual home, she had a creative idea. She would use many of the old materials that she collected in the home's design. For example, she used old car parts in the front door and tire rubber as the roof. She also used the door of an old car as part of a wall, so she can still lower the window!

Wayne and Cate are a couple from the U.S. state of Montana. They wanted a new home that wasn't too expensive. Their solution was simple – they built their own home. They recycled and used 250 old tires as the base of the house and old glass for the windows. They even used 13,000 empty soda cans in the house. Their home also has large windows and lots of plants and flowers. Solar energy keeps the house warm, even on cold days.

C Read the article again. Answer the questions.

1 What warms the inside of Shoichi's home? _____
2 What would Shoichi like to be able to do? _____
3 What creative idea did Ruth have? _____
4 Where are there car parts in Ruth's home? _____
5 Why did Wayne and Cate build their own home? _____
6 What did Wayne and Cate use to build their home? _____

D **PAIR WORK** Have you heard of or seen any unique homes or buildings? Were they environmentally friendly? Tell your partner.

2 Listening Award winners

A 🎧 **Listen to the conversations about two award winners, Gabriela McCall and Tayler McGillis. Who do the phrases below describe? Write T (Tayler) or G (Gabriela).**

1. ___T___ raised money for local charities.
2. _____ is a student in Puerto Rico.
3. _____ won an award at age 12.
4. _____ collects and recycles cans.
5. _____ helps birds.
6. _____ teaches children.
7. _____ speaks at schools about recycling.
8. _____ took photos to start a project.

B 🎧 **Listen again. Correct the false sentences.**

1. Tayler raised more than ~~$900~~ for local charities. _____$9,000_____
2. Tayler's new goal is to collect 175,000 bottles every year. _____
3. Gabriela's project helps protect the ocean for birds in Puerto Rico. _____
4. Gabriela teaches children about recycling so that they respect the environment. _____

3 Writing and speaking Local concerns

A **Write a letter to a local official about an environmental problem in your community. Use the questions and the model to help you.**

- What is the problem?
- Who or what does the problem affect?
- Who or what is causing it?
- What's a solution to the problem?

Dear City Councilman,

I am a student. I am writing to tell you about the amount of noise near our school. There is a lot of construction work and traffic near our school. It is very difficult for us to study and learn during the day.

I have an idea for a possible solution to this problem. If . . .

B **GROUP WORK** **Share your letters. Do you think the solutions will solve the problems? Can you offer other solutions?**

C **CLASS ACTIVITY** **What are the most important concerns in your community? Who else can you write to or talk to about your concerns?**

I can discuss solutions to problems. ✓

Wrap-up

1 Quick pair review

Lesson A `Brainstorm!`

Make a list of environmentally friendly products. How many do you know?
You have two minutes.

Lesson B `Do you remember?`

Is the sentence giving an approximate answer, or is it avoiding answering?
Write AP (approximate answer) or AV (avoiding answering). You have one minute.

How much did your car cost?		How much trash do you throw away a week?	
I'd say about $3,000.	_____	I'd rather not answer that.	_____
I'd prefer not to say.	_____	I'd rather not say.	_____
I'd say maybe $6,000.	_____	Probably about five bags.	_____

Lesson C `Give your opinion!`

What do you think? Complete the sentences together. You have three minutes.

1 Our city will get cleaner if _____

2 If our school uses solar energy, _____

3 If we eat organic food, _____

4 We could recycle more if _____

Lesson D `Find out!`

Who is one person you know who does each thing? You have two minutes.

● Who uses environmentally friendly products at home?

● Who take public transportation to school?

● Who has taught you about an environmental issue?

A: *My aunt has solar panels on the roof of her house.*

B: *My father uses compact fluorescent lightbulbs.*

2 In the real world

How can we solve this? Go online and find information in English that gives
solutions to one of these problems. Then write about them.

pollution from cars	pollution from factories
global warming	too much garbage

On Pollution Problem

If more people have hybrid cars, there will be less pollution.
People can also carpool. If we share rides, there will be fewer
cars on the road. Also, if we . . .

82

9 Relationships

Lesson A
- Relationship behaviors
- Expressions with infinitives

Lesson B
- Apologizing
- Accepting an apology

Lesson C
- Inseparable phrasal verbs
- Modals for speculating

Lesson D
- Reading "Addy's Advice"
- Writing: A piece of advice

Warm Up

A What is the relationship between the people? Number the pictures.

1 brother and sister   2 neighbors   3 co-workers   4 friends

B What do you think is happening in each picture? Do they all have good relationships?

A Healthy relationships

1 **Vocabulary** Relationship behaviors

A 🎧 **Match the words and the sentences. Then listen and check your answers.**

1	apologize _____	a.	No! I'm not listening to you.
2	argue _____	b.	I think we really need to talk about it.
3	communicate _____	c.	I'm really sorry. I didn't mean to hurt your feelings.

4	compromise _____	d.	I know you're sorry. It's OK.
5	criticize _____	e.	Why don't I wash the dishes and you do the laundry?
6	forgive _____	f.	You're being unfair. It's your turn to take out the garbage.

7	gossip _____	g.	I told her I liked her new dress, but I didn't.
8	judge _____	h.	Others may disagree, but I think what you said was awful.
9	lie _____	i.	Did you hear about Wendy? You'll never guess what I heard.

B **PAIR WORK** **Which actions from Part A should people do to have healthy relationships? Which shouldn't they do? Discuss your ideas.**

2 **Language in context** Relationship tips

A 🎧 **Read the relationship tips. Why is it a bad idea to criticize someone in front of others?**

4:21PM

5 Tips for happy and healthy relationships

1. It's important to talk. It's good to communicate openly and listen carefully to others.

2. It's not a good idea to criticize someone in front of others. This can embarrass the person.

3. It's helpful to compromise in any relationship. It's not good to argue about little things.

4. It's good to forgive someone who apologizes. It's not easy to say you're sorry.

5. If you have a problem in a relationship, it's helpful to discuss it. Don't keep things inside.

B **What about you? Do you agree with all the tips? Why or why not?**

3 Grammar 🎧 Expressions with infinitives

> *Use infinitives after It's + an adjective.*
>
> It's good **to forgive** someone.   It's not good **to argue**.
>
> It's important **to talk**.   It's never helpful **to judge** someone.
>
> *You can also use infinitives after It's + a noun phrase.*
>
> It's a good idea **to accept** an apology.   It's not a good idea **to criticize** someone.

A Circle the infinitives for the best relationship advice. Then compare with a partner.

1 It's important **to lie** / **to communicate** in a relationship.

2 It's helpful **to share** / **to forget** your feelings when you have a problem.

3 It's nice **to gossip** / **to think** about other people before making decisions.

4 It's a good idea **to judge** / **to meet** new people.

5 It's useful **to discuss** / **to accept** problems.

6 It's not a good idea **to argue** / **to compromise** with your friends a lot.

B PAIR WORK Complete the sentences with your own ideas. Use *It's* expressions. Then discuss them.

1 _____ to be a reliable friend.

2 _____ to be honest with your parents.

3 _____ to apologize to someone but not really mean it.

4 _____ to say something if a friend is gossiping about you.

4 Pronunciation Sentence stress

A 🎧 Listen and repeat. Notice the stress on the important words in the sentences.

It's **important** to **talk**.   It's **not good** to **argue** about **little things**.

B 🎧 Listen to the sentences. Underline the stressed words.

It's helpful to compromise.   It's not easy to say you're sorry.

5 Speaking Good advice?

A PAIR WORK Choose a relationship from the list below. Then make a list of the five most important tips to make the relationship happy and healthy. Discuss your ideas.

best friends	classmates
a brother and sister	a married couple
a child and parent	a teacher and student

B GROUP WORK Share your tips with another pair. What's the best piece of advice you heard?

6 Keep talking!

Go to page 141 for more practice.

I can discuss what's important in relationships. ✓

B I'm really sorry.

1 Interactions Apologizing

A Is it difficult for you to say you're sorry? Can you remember the last thing you apologized for?

B 🎧 Listen to the conversation. What excuse does Susan give Gina? Then practice the conversation.

Gina   Hello?

Susan   Gina?

Gina   Yeah.

Susan   Hi. It's Susan.

Gina   Hi, Susan.

Susan   Listen, I know I missed your party last night. I'm sorry.

Gina   Oh, that's OK. Is everything OK?

Susan   Yeah, but you'll never believe what happened. It's kind of embarrassing. I mixed up the date.

Gina   What do you mean?

Susan   I thought the party was on the 31st, not the 30th.

Gina   Oh, I see.

Susan   So, how was the party?

Gina   It was great. But we missed you!

C 🎧 Read the expressions below. Complete each box with a similar expression from the conversation. Then listen and check your answers.

Apologizing
_____
I'm really sorry.
My apologies.

Accepting an apology
_____
Don't worry about it.
There's no need to apologize.

D Number the sentences from 1 to 7. Then practice with a partner.

_____ **A** I'm really sorry I didn't meet you at the café yesterday.

_____ **A** Hi. It's Greg.

_____ **A** Well, the repairs will be very expensive.

_____ **A** My car broke down, and I forgot my phone.

_____ **B** Is your car OK?

_____ **B** Don't worry about it.

_____ **B** Oh. Hi, Greg.

86

2 Listening What happened?

A 🎧 Listen to four people apologize over the phone. Where did they *not* go?
Number the pictures from 1 to 4.

B 🎧 Listen again. Complete the excuses with the correct information.

1 I was at the _____ and completely forgot the _____ .

2 I washed my _____ last night, and the _____ was in my pocket.

3 I was out of _____ . My grandmother was in the _____ .

4 I'm in a _____ at work. I can't _____ right now.

C **PAIR WORK** Are all the excuses good ones? Would you accept each person's apology?
Discuss your ideas.

3 Speaking Explain yourself!

A Read the situations. Write an excuse for each one. Be creative!

Situations	Excuses
You are 30 minutes late for your own wedding.	
You missed your dentist appointment.	
You didn't bring your résumé to a job interview.	
You forgot to pick up your friend.	
You didn't do your English homework.	
You broke your classmate's cell phone.	

B **PAIR WORK** Role-play the situations. Then change roles.

Student A: Apologize to Student B for each situation in Part A. Then make an excuse.

Student B: Ask Student A to explain each situation. Then accept the apology.

I can apologize and give excuses. ✓

I can accept an apology. ✓

C That can't be the problem.

1 Vocabulary Inseparable phrasal verbs

A 🎧 Match the sentences. Then listen and check your answers.

1	It's awful when people **break up**. _____	a.	They should call before they visit.
2	I need friends that I can **count on**. _____	b.	It's always better to stay together.
3	It's not nice when friends just **drop by**. _____	c.	My best friends are all reliable.

4	My family and I **get along** well. _____	d.	They can be so immature.
5	My friends and I love to **get together**. _____	e.	We meet every Saturday.
6	Most teenagers need to **grow up**. _____	f.	We hardly ever argue.

7	People used to **pick on** me in class. _____	g.	I sometimes see them at the coffee shop.
8	I love to **run into** old friends. _____	h.	I'm just like her.
9	I **take after** my mother. _____	i.	They were mean to me.

B PAIR WORK Which sentences do you agree with or are true for you? Tell your partner.

A: I agree that it's awful when people break up, but I disagree that it's always better to stay together.

B: I agree with you. Some people shouldn't stay together when they argue a lot.

2 Conversation He must be really busy.

A 🎧 Listen to the conversation. What is Evan probably doing right now?

Ryan   My friend Evan never seems to have time for me these days. I just can't count on him anymore.

Katie   Well, he started a new job, right? He must be really busy.

Ryan   Yeah, I'm sure he is. But he used to drop by or call me all the time.

Katie   He might be feeling stressed out from the job. Or he could be upset with you about something.

Ryan   No, that can't be the problem. I haven't done anything wrong. I think I'd better call him.

Katie   Yeah, I think you should.

Ryan   OK. . . . Well, there's no answer.

Katie   He must still be sleeping. It's only 6:30!

B 🎧 Listen to Ryan call Evan later in the day. What was the real problem with Evan?

3 Grammar 🎧 Modals for speculating

Speculating with more certainty	Speculating with less certainty
He **must be** really busy. He started a new job.	He **could be** upset about something. Maybe you did something to him.
He **must not leave** his house very often. He always seems to be busy.	He **may not like** his new job. I haven't heard how he likes it.
He **can't be** upset with me. I haven't done anything to him.	He **might be feeling** stressed out. His new job may be a lot of work.

A Circle the correct words. Then compare with a partner.

1 I don't know his weekend plans. He **must / could** drop by on Saturday.

2 She didn't say much on the phone to him. They **must not / might** be getting along.

3 They **must / may not** come to the party. They're going out to dinner that night.

4 She **can't / could** take after her father. She's really tall, but he's pretty short.

5 You're coughing and sneezing so much. You **must / must not** be getting sick.

6 They **can't / might** be tired. Maybe they stayed up late to study for the test.

B Read the situations. Complete the sentences with your own ideas. Then compare with a partner.

1 Pamela and Miguel don't get along anymore. She doesn't want to talk about it.

Pamela must _____.

2 Jeff just ran into his college friend Mary. He hasn't seen her for 20 years.

Jeff could _____.

3 Luis and Teresa arranged to get together at a restaurant, but she never came.

Teresa may not _____.

4 Brian dropped by and asked to copy your homework. You're not going to give it to him.

Brian might _____.

4 Speaking Look around!

A PAIR WORK Look around the classroom. Speculate about your classmates.

A: I think Tom must be playing tennis later. He has his tennis racket with him today.

B: And Carmen might be happy about something. She's smiling a lot.

B CLASS ACTIVITY Were your speculations correct? Ask your classmates.

A: Tom, I see you have your tennis racket. Are you playing tennis later?

B: Actually, no. I played before class.

5 Keep talking!

Go to pages 142-143 for more practice.

I can speculate about people. ✓

D Getting advice

1 Reading 🎧

A Do you ever ask for advice on the radio, TV or through social media? What kind of problems do people usually ask for help with? Do you think they are good places to ask for advice?

B Read the first few sentences of each email sent to the radio show *Addy's Advice*. Who does each person have a problem with?

Addy's Advice 🏠 ✉ 💬 ☰

1. I have a big problem. It's my best friend. She doesn't really have any time for me these days. I call her, and she can't talk. I text her, and she doesn't answer right away. I think it's because of her cat, Peaches. She got this little cat for her 30th birthday, and now she takes it everywhere. She even dresses it in little sweaters and hats. I don't know what to do. Is it possible to be jealous of a cat? **– T.J.**

2. There's this new person at work. She works next to me and we get along, but she's always asking me to do things for her. For example, she asks me to get her coffee when I get some for myself. Or she drops by and asks me to copy things for her when she's "busy." She's not my boss! Should I just refuse to do things for her? I want to be nice, but I have to do my own work. Can you help me, please? **– Marcy**

3. My little brother is driving me crazy. I'm 15, and he's 10. He has his own friends, but he won't leave me and my friends alone. They come over a lot to study or just watch TV. He bothers me and sometimes tells my friends things that are personal about me. Maybe he just wants attention, but it's very annoying. He should just grow up! Anyway, I told my mom and dad, but they say I need to solve the problem. **– Kathy**

4. I'm a neat person, and I used to live alone. I got a roommate a few months ago to help with the rent. The problem is, my roommate is not like me at all. He never does any chores around the house. He just sits around playing video games and watching TV. The apartment is always a mess, and I'm the one who has to clean it up. I can't count on him for anything. Should I just clean the apartment myself? This is a big problem for me. **– Daniel**

C Read the emails again. Who is each question about? Check (✓) the correct answers.

Who...?	T.J.	Marcy	Kathy	Daniel
lives with a messy person				
is a teenager				
is jealous of an animal				
is doing someone else's work				
lived alone last year				
mentions parents in the letter				

D **PAIR WORK** Have you ever had similar problems? What did you do about them? Tell your partner.

2 Listening On the air

A 🎧 **Listen to the radio show *Addy's Advice*. What advice does Addy give to each person from Exercise 1? Check (✓) the correct answers.**

1 ☐ Show interest in the cat.
   ☐ Get a cat of your own.

2 ☐ Write your co-worker a note.
   ☐ Ask your co-worker to do things.

3 ☐ Go to someone else's house.
   ☐ Remind your parents of the situation.

4 ☐ Throw the roommate out.
   ☐ Communicate.

B 🎧 **Listen again. Which statement does Addy probably agree or disagree with? Write A (agree) or D (disagree).**

1 People never lose interest in things over time. _____

2 Most people have problems with co-workers at some time. _____

3 Parents don't always need to solve their children's problems. _____

4 Look for a new roommate if you have a problem. _____

3 Writing A piece of advice

A Choose an email from Exercise 1. Think of three pieces of advice.

B Write an email giving advice. Use the model and your ideas from Part A to help you.

C GROUP WORK Share your emails. Do you agree with the advice? What other advice can you give? Discuss your ideas.

> Dear T.J.,
>
> I read your email, and I understand your problem. It *is* possible to be jealous of a cat! I think it's important to find things that you can *do* with your friend and Peaches. It's a good idea to…

4 Speaking Take it or leave it.

A Imagine you have two relationship problems. Write two sentences about each one. Be creative!

B GROUP WORK Share your imaginary problems. Your group gives advice. Take turns.

A: I have a problem. My friends never remember my birthday. I always remember theirs!

B: It's a good idea to help them remember. Why not send them reminders?

C GROUP WORK Whose advice do you think you'd follow? Why? Tell your group.

> 1. My friends never remember my birthday. I always remember theirs!
> 2. My parents don't trust me. I need to call them every three hours.

I can give advice about relationships. ✓

Wrap-up

1 Quick pair review

Lesson A `Brainstorm!`

Make a list of tips for healthy family relationships. How many can you think of?
You have five minutes.

Lesson B `Test your partner!`

Apologize to your partner for three different things. Can your partner accept your
apologies in three different ways? Take turns. You have two minutes.

Lesson C `Guess!`

Speculate about a celebrity, but don't say his or her name! Can your partner
guess who it is? Take turns. You have two minutes.

A: This person might win an award for his new movie.

B: Is it...?

Lesson D `Find out!`

What is the best relationship advice your partner has ever received? Who gave the
advice? You have two minutes.

2 In the real world

What advice do the experts give? Go online and find advice in English about one
of these topics. Then write about it.

a jealous friend	a neighbor's noisy dog
a friend who talks too much	an annoying boss
a lazy husband or wife	an inconsiderate neighbor

Dealing with Jealous Friends

I found a website that gives advice about jealous friends. If
you have a jealous friend, try to find out why the friend is
jealous. Try to understand how your friend feels. It's a good
idea to tell your friend about a time when you felt jealous,
too. That way she will not feel alone or embarrassed. Tell
your friend what you did to feel better. Another piece of
advice on the website is ...

10 Living your life

Warm Up

A Look at the pictures. What have the people accomplished?

B What are some of your accomplishments? What other things would you like to accomplish in your life?

93

A He taught himself.

1 Vocabulary Qualities for success

A 🎧 **Match the words and their meanings. Then listen and check your answers.**

1	bravery ___	a.	the ability to develop original ideas
2	confidence ___	b.	the belief that you can succeed
3	creativity ___	c.	a commitment to something
4	dedication ___	d.	the quality of showing no fear

5	enthusiasm ___	e.	the ability to change easily
6	flexibility ___	f.	a strong interest in something
7	talent ___	g.	the ability to make good decisions
8	wisdom ___	h.	the natural ability to do things well

B 🎧 **Complete the chart with the correct adjective forms for the nouns. Then listen and check your answers.**

Noun	Adjective	Noun	Adjective
bravery	brave	enthusiasm	
confidence		flexibility	
creativity		talent	
dedication		wisdom	

C **PAIR WORK** **Which qualities in Part A do you think people are born with? Which do they develop from experience or by watching others? Discuss your ideas.**

2 Language in context A success story

A 🎧 **Read the story of Yong-eun Yang. What did he do in 2009?**

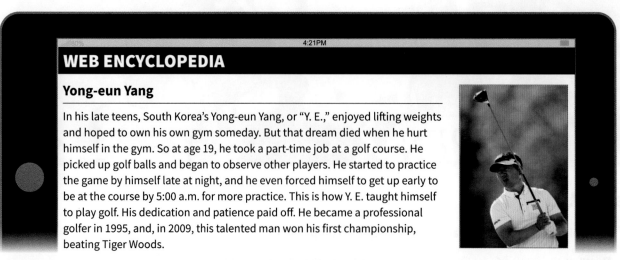

WEB ENCYCLOPEDIA

Yong-eun Yang

In his late teens, South Korea's Yong-eun Yang, or "Y. E.," enjoyed lifting weights and hoped to own his own gym someday. But that dream died when he hurt himself in the gym. So at age 19, he took a part-time job at a golf course. He picked up golf balls and began to observe other players. He started to practice the game by himself late at night, and he even forced himself to get up early to be at the course by 5:00 a.m. for more practice. This is how Y. E. taught himself to play golf. His dedication and patience paid off. He became a professional golfer in 1995, and, in 2009, this talented man won his first championship, beating Tiger Woods.

B **What other qualities for success do you think Y.E. has?**

94

3 Grammar 🎧 Reflexive pronouns

	Personal pronouns	Reflexive pronouns
Use reflexive pronouns when the subject and object of a sentence refer to the same person or thing. I hurt **myself** at work. He taught **himself** to play golf. They consider **themselves** brave. By *with a reflexive pronoun means "alone."* She traveled **by herself** to the United States. Do you like to practice with another person or **by yourself**?	I you he she it we you they	myself yourself himself herself itself ourselves yourselves themselves

Complete the sentences with the correct reflexive pronouns. Then compare with a partner.

1 I drew a picture of _____ in art class.

2 I like your new hairstyle. Did you cut it _____?

3 I think you and Joe can fix the sink _____. You don't need to hire a plumber.

4 They had a great time. They really enjoyed _____.

5 My brother doesn't consider _____ brave, but he is.

6 Heather wrote that by _____. Nobody helped her.

7 We taught _____ Spanish before we moved to Peru.

8 I hurt _____ at the gym last week. My arm still hurts.

9 I took a trip by _____. It helped me be more confident.

4 Pronunciation Stress shifts

🎧 **Listen and repeat. Notice the stress shifts when some words change from nouns to adjectives.**

crea**ti**vity	dedi**ca**tion	enthu**si**asm	flexi**bi**lity
cre**a**tive	**de**dicated	enthusi**as**tic	**flex**ible

5 Speaking Self talk

A PAIR WORK **Interview your partner. Ask questions for more information. Take notes.**

- Have you ever hurt yourself?
- Do you consider yourself brave?
- Have you ever traveled by yourself?
- Have you ever taught yourself something?
- Are you enjoying yourself in this class?
- Do you consider yourself a flexible person?

B PAIR WORK **Tell another classmate about your partner.**

"William hurt himself once. He broke his foot."

6 Keep talking!

Go to page 144 for more practice.

I can talk about myself and my experiences. ✅

B I'll give it some thought.

1 Interactions Giving and considering advice

A What do you do if you have too much work or studying to do? Do you talk to anyone?

B 🎧 Listen to the conversation. What is Bryan thinking about doing? Then practice the conversation.

Marta	What's wrong, Bryan?
Bryan	Well, my job is just really stressful right now. My boss just seems to give me more and more work. It's not fair.
Marta	That's not good.
Bryan	Actually, I'm thinking about quitting and looking for another job.
Marta	Really? I wouldn't recommend that.
Bryan	Why not?
Marta	Well, because you may not find something better. And that would just give you more stress. Have you thought about talking to your boss?
Bryan	Not really.
Marta	Why don't you try that? Maybe there is something he can do.
Bryan	I'll see.

C 🎧 Read the expressions below. Complete each box with a similar expression from the conversation. Then listen and check your answers.

Advising against something
_____
I don't think you should do that.
I'm not sure that's the best idea.

Considering advice
_____
I'll think about it.
I'll give it some thought.

D How would you respond? Write A (advise against it) or C (consider it). Then practice with a partner.

1 I think you should call the doctor. _____
2 I plan to study all night before my test. _____
3 I recommend that you stay home tomorrow if you don't feel well. _____
4 I think you should visit your grandmother this weekend. _____
5 I'm going to paint my house bright pink. _____
6 I'm not going to class tomorrow because I want to watch a soccer game. _____

2 Listening Maybe I'll do that.

A 🎧 Listen to Tim give advice to three friends. What is each friend's problem? Check (✓) the correct answers.

Problems	Recommendations
1 ☐ She needs to get a full-time job. ☐ She wants to take more classes. ☐ She's thinking about quitting her job. ☐ She's not going to graduate.	
2 ☐ He doesn't have the money. ☐ He doesn't have a credit card. ☐ The leather jacket doesn't fit. ☐ His friend won't lend him any money.	
3 ☐ She takes too many breaks. ☐ She can't do a math problem. ☐ She drank too much coffee. ☐ Tim is driving her crazy.	

B 🎧 Listen again. What does Tim tell each friend to do? Complete the chart with his recommendations.

3 Speaking Think about it!

A Imagine your friend wants to do the things below. What advice would you give? Write notes.

- Your friend wants to buy a new, expensive car. He doesn't have the money, and he doesn't know how to drive!

- Your friend wants to take two more classes. He's already taking five classes, and he has a part-time job!

- Your friend wants to go camping in the mountains by himself for a week. He's never gone camping before!

B **PAIR WORK** Role-play the situations in Part A. Then change roles.

Student A: Imagine you want to do the things in Part A. Tell Student B what you want to do and why. Consider his or her advice.

Student B: Advise Student A against doing the things in Part A and explain why. Recommend something else. Use your ideas from Part A.

A: I saw this really awesome car yesterday! I think I'm going to buy it.

B: I'm not sure that's the best idea.

A: Why not?

I can advise against something. ✓
I can consider advice. ✓

C What would you do?

1 Vocabulary Separable phrasal verbs

A 🎧 Match the phrasal verbs and their meanings. Then listen and check your answers.

1	He won't talk about his job, so I don't **bring** it **up**. _____	a. donate
2	I got a bad grade on this essay. I need to **do** it **over**. _____	b. return money
3	I don't need these books. I might **give** them **away**. _____	c. mention
4	This is Lynn's camera. I need to **give** it **back**. _____	d. do again
5	Paul lent me some money. I need to **pay** him **back**. _____	e. return

6	Which one is Susan? Can you **point** her **out**? _____	f. do later
7	We can't have this meeting now. Let's **put** it **off**. _____	g. identify
8	This is serious. We need to **talk** it **over**. _____	h. not accept
9	I may buy that car, but I want to **try** it **out** first. _____	i. use
10	I have a job offer, but I plan to **turn** it **down**. _____	j. discuss

B **PAIR WORK** What have you done over, talked over, paid back, tried out, or put off recently? Tell your partner.

A: *Have you done anything over recently?*

B: *Yes, I have. I did my English homework over last night. I made a lot of mistakes the first time!*

2 Conversation I'm kind of broke.

A 🎧 Listen to the conversation. What is Lucia thinking about doing?

Elliot	I really like your camera.
Lucia	Actually, it's my friend Ben's. I'm just trying it out this week. I need to give it back to him tomorrow.
Elliot	It looks really expensive.
Lucia	It is. I'm thinking about buying one, but I can't right now.
Elliot	Why not?
Lucia	Well, I'm kind of broke. If I had more money, I'd buy it.
Elliot	It would be nice to be rich, wouldn't it?
Lucia	Tell me about it. What would you do if you were rich?
Elliot	Hmm . . . If I were rich, I'd travel. I'd give some money away, too.
Lucia	That's nice.

B 🎧 Listen to the rest of the conversation. Why does Lucia want a camera?

3 Grammar 🎧 Second conditional

> *Second conditional sentences describe "unreal" or imaginary situations. Use a past tense verb in the* if *clause (the condition). Use* would *in the main clause.*
> What **would** you **do** if you **had** more money?
>   If I **had** more money, I **would buy** a camera.
>
> *Use* were *for the past tense of* be *in the condition.*
> **Would** you **travel** if you **were** rich?
>   Yes, I **would**.   No, I **wouldn't**.
>   Yes. If I **were** rich, I'**d travel** a lot.   No. I **wouldn't travel** a lot if I **were** rich.

A Complete the conversations with the correct words. Then compare with a partner.

1 A What _____ you _____ (do) if you suddenly _____
   (become) rich?

   B I _____ (quit) my job. Then I _____ (travel) for a few months.

2 A If a teacher _____ (give) you a good grade by mistake, what _____
   you _____ (do)?

   B I _____ (not / feel) right about it. I _____ (point) out the mistake.

3 A How _____ you _____ (feel) if a friend _____ (call)
   you late at night?

   B I _____ (be) surprised, but I _____ (not / feel) angry.

4 A If you _____ (have) a relationship problem, who _____ you
   _____ (talk) to?

   B I _____ (talk) about the problem with my best friend.

B PAIR WORK Ask and answer the questions in Part A. Answer with your own information.

4 Speaking What would you do?

A PAIR WORK Discuss the questions. Take notes.

- Where would you go if you had a lot of money?
- What would you give away if you were rich?
- What would you do if you saw your teacher or your boss at the supermarket?
- When would you turn down a job offer?
- Would you point out a mistake if a classmate made one? Why or why not?
- What would you do over if you had the chance?

B GROUP WORK Share your ideas with another pair. Are your ideas similar or different?

5 Keep talking!

Go to page 145 for more practice.

D What an accomplishment!

1 Reading 🎧

A What do you think it would be like to walk across your country? Why?

B Read the interview. Why did Mary and Etsuko often have to walk between 30 and 40 kilometers a day?

A Walk Across Japan

Mary King and Etsuko Shimabukuro completed a 7,974-kilometer walk across Japan. Mary takes our questions about their incredible accomplishment.

Why did you walk across Japan?
The mapmaker Ino Tadataka *inspired* me. He spent 17 years *on and off* walking through Japan. He drew the country's first real maps.

How long did it take?
A year and a half. We walked from the island of Hokkaido, in the north, down to Okinawa. In Hokkaido, we walked about 40 kilometers a day, and on the other islands, about 30. We often had no choice about the distance because we had to find a place to sleep.

Describe a typical day.
There really wasn't one, but we tried to start by 7:00 a.m. and walk for 10 to 12 hours. Sometimes we had breakfast on the road. We had to be careful in Hokkaido because the bears there could smell our food. We saw bears twice, which was terrifying!

Did you walk every day?
No. We needed to do our laundry, check our email, and rest. Also, I wanted to interview people for my blog.

What were some of the best parts?
There were many! We stayed in a *haunted* guesthouse, walked on fire at a festival, and visited many wonderful hot springs.

Any low points?
You know, overall, we really enjoyed ourselves, but there were a lot of aches and pains along the way. The traffic could be scary because there weren't always sidewalks for *pedestrians*.

Did you ever think about *giving up*?
No, we never wanted to stop. Actually, I was sad when it ended. I wanted to walk from Okinawa back to Tokyo, but Etsuko said we had to accept that we accomplished our goal. It was time to go home.

Would you do it over again?
Definitely. I'd love to *retrace* our steps when I'm 80. But I've also set myself the goal of walking across the U.K. or India someday.

C Find the words in *italics* in the article. What do they mean? Write the words next to the correct definitions.

1 inhabited by ghosts ___haunted___

2 quitting _____

3 people who walk _____

4 go back over a route again _____

5 with breaks _____

6 gave someone an idea _____

D **PAIR WORK** How would you describe Mary's personality? Do you know anyone like her?

2 Listening Can I ask you . . .?

A 🎧 Listen to four people talk about their biggest accomplishments this year. Write the accomplishments in the chart.

Accomplishments		Qualities for success
1		
2		
3		
4		

B 🎧 Listen again. What quality led to each person's success? Complete the chart.

C PAIR WORK Who do you think had the biggest accomplishment? Why? Discuss your ideas.

3 Writing An accomplishment

A Write a paragraph about something you accomplished in your lifetime. Use the questions and the model to help you.

- What did you accomplish?
- Why did you decide to do it?
- How did you accomplish it?
- What was challenging about it?
- Why was it important?

B GROUP WORK Share your paragraphs. How are your accomplishments similar or different?

A Healthy Change

I decided that I wanted to change something at our school. A lot of the vending machines had very unhealthy food, like chocolate, candy, and potato chips. Students wanted healthier food like fruits and yogurt. So I asked students and teachers to sign a petition to get healthier food. It was difficult at first . . .

4 Speaking What have you done?

CLASS ACTIVITY Find people who have done these things. Write their names and ask questions for more information.

Find someone who has . . .	Name	Extra information
helped someone with a challenging task		
won an award for doing something		
learned a new skill outside of school		
solved a problem at school, home, or work		
used technology to improve his or her English		

I can ask and talk about accomplishments.

101

Wrap-up

1 Quick pair review

Lesson A Test your partner!

Say three personal pronouns. Can your partner use the correct reflexive pronouns in sentences? Take turns. You have two minutes.

A: He.

B: Himself. My neighbor introduced himself to me yesterday.

Lesson B Do you remember?

Which sentences are advising against something? Check (✓) the correct answers. You have one minute.

- ☐ I don't think you should do that.
- ☐ Please don't worry about it.
- ☐ I'm not sure that's the best idea.
- ☐ I'll give it some thought.
- ☐ I'd rather not answer that.
- ☐ I wouldn't recommend that.

Lesson C Find out!

What is one thing both you and your partner would do in each situation? You have three minutes.

- Where would you go if you won a free vacation?
- What would you buy if you received money for your birthday?
- What would you do if you lost your cell phone?

Lesson D Brainstorm!

Make a list of accomplishments. How many can you think of? You have two minutes.

2 In the real world

Which country would you like to travel across? Go online and find information in English about one of these trips or your own idea. Then answer the questions and write about it.

a car trip across the United States	a train trip across Canada
a bike trip across France	a walking trip across England

- How far is it?
- How much would it cost?
- Where would you stay?
- How long would it take?
- What would you need to take?

A Road Trip in the U.S.A.

I'd take a car trip across the United States. I'd start in Ocean City, Maryland, and drive to San Francisco, California. The trip is about 3,000 miles. The first place I would stop is . . .

11 Music

Lesson A	Lesson B	Lesson C	Lesson D
● Compound adjectives ● Past passive	● Giving instructions	● Verb and noun formation ● Present perfect with *yet* and *already*	● Reading "A Guide to Breaking into the Music Business" ● Writing: A music review

Music Sales in the U.S.A.

jazz, 2%
latin 2%
other 15%
classical 2%
rock 25%
punk 3%
R & B 7%
stage and screen 7%
hip hop/ rap 9%
country 14%
pop 14%

"Source: www.statista.com, 2017"

Warm Up

A Label the pictures with the correct types of music from the chart.

B What do you think are the most popular kinds of music where you live?
What's your favorite kind of music? What's your least favorite? Why?

A Music trivia

1 Vocabulary Compound adjectives

A 🎧 **Complete the compound adjectives with the correct participles. Then listen and check your answers.**

Compound adjective		Present
award-_winning_	video	selling
best-_____	artist	winning ✓
nice-_____	voice	breaking
record-_____	hit	sounding

Compound adjective		Past participle
high-_____	ticket	downloaded
oddly _____	group	priced
often-_____	performer	named
well-_____	singer	known

B **PAIR WORK** **Ask and answer questions with each phrase in Part A. Answer with your own ideas.**

A: *Can you name an award-winning video?*

B: *Yes. Michael Jackson's video for "Thriller" won a lot of awards.*

2 Language in context Musical firsts

A 🎧 **Read about these musical firsts. Which musical firsts involved downloading?**

Milestones in Music History

The first rap recording was made by the Sugarhill Gang. In 1979, the band's song "Rapper's Delight" became the first rap song to make the U.S. pop charts.

The song "Crazy" by Gnarls Barkley was leaked in 2005, months before its release. When it was finally released in March 2006, it became the first song to reach number one from downloaded sales.

The band Radiohead was the first to sell their album online for whatever people wanted to pay. Over a million albums were downloaded before the CD was released in December 2007.

The well-known band Aerosmith was the first to have a video game created around their music. People can play the guitar and sing along to 41 of their songs. The game was released in June 2008.

B **What else do you know about these musical firsts? Do you know of any others?**

"The band Run-DMC also recorded the song 'Rapper's Delight.'"

3 Grammar 🎧 Past passive

The passive voice places the focus of a sentence on the receiver of an action instead of the doer of the action.

Active voice (simple past)
Fans **downloaded** <u>over a million albums</u>.

Passive voice (past of be + *past participle)*
<u>Over a million albums</u> **were downloaded**.

Use the passive voice when the doer of the action is not known or not important.
The game **was released** in 2008.

When the doer of the action is important to know, use the passive voice with by.
The first rap recording **was made** <u>by</u> the Sugarhill Gang.

A Complete the sentences with the past passive forms of the verbs.
Then compare with a partner.

1 All of the high-priced tickets to the concert _____ (sell) online.

2 The best-selling artists of the year _____ (give) a special award.

3 The singer's record-breaking hit _____ (write) by her mother.

4 The performer's biggest hit song _____ (use) in a TV commercial.

5 The band's award-winning video _____ (see) by millions of people.

6 The songs on her album _____ (play) with traditional instruments.

B PAIR WORK Say the trivia about the music group the Beatles. Your partner changes the sentences to use the past passive. Take turns.

1 In 1960, John Lennon suggested the name "the Beatles."

2 Ringo Starr replaced the original drummer, Peter Best, in 1962.

3 Paul McCartney wrote "Hey Jude" for John Lennon's son Julian.

4 Many people called George Harrison "the quiet Beatle."

5 *Rolling Stone* magazine chose the Beatles as the best artists of all time.

A: In 1960, John Lennon suggested the name "the Beatles."

B: In 1960, the name "the Beatles" was suggested by John Lennon.

4 Speaking Name it!

A Write three sentences in the past passive about the same song, singer, musician, band, or album, but don't use the name!

B GROUP WORK Share your sentences. Your group guesses the name of the song, singer, musician, band, or album. Take turns.

1. This singer's first album was called The Fame.

2. She was born in New York City.

3. She was made famous by her music and fashion statements.

(answer: Lady Gaga)

5 Keep talking!

Go to page 146 for more practice.

I can **talk about music.** ✓

B The first thing you do is . . .

1 Interactions Giving instructions

A What kinds of things do you use a computer for? How did you learn to do those things?

B 🎧 Listen to the conversation. What steps does Amy follow to make a video playlist? Then practice the conversation.

Tyler	What are you doing, Mom?
Amy	I'm trying to make a video playlist, but I'm not having much luck.
Tyler	Let's see. First you need to create an account by typing in your information.
Amy	OK. Thanks. Now what?
Tyler	Next, search for the video you want to be first on your playlist.
Amy:	All right. . . . Ah, here we go. How do I add it to a playlist?
Tyler	Under the video, click *Add to . . .* and then choose *Create new playlist*. That's where you'll name your playlist and choose your privacy setting.
Amy	Oh, look at that. Is that it?
Tyler	Well, no. Finally, click *CREATE*.

C 🎧 Read the expressions below. Complete each box with a similar expression from the conversation. Then listen and check your answers.

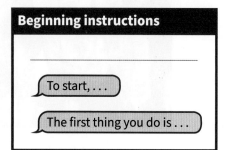

Beginning instructions

To start, . . .

The first thing you do is . . .

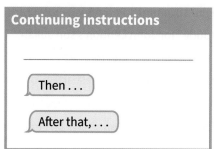

Continuing instructions

Then . . .

After that, . . .

Ending instructions

To finish, . . .

The last thing you do is . . .

D **PAIR WORK** Number the instructions from 1 to 5. Then have a conversation like the one in Part B.

How to download a ring tone:

_____ Click the *set ringtone* button to make the song your ring tone.

_____ Browse or search for a song in the app.

_____ Enjoy your new ringtone whenever your friends call you.

_____ Download the song you want to be your ringtone.

_____ Download a free ringtone app on your smartphone.

2 Listening How does it work?

A 🎧 Listen to people give instructions on how to use three different machines. Number the machines from 1 to 3. There is one extra machine.

B 🎧 Listen again. Each person makes one mistake when giving instructions. Write the mistakes.

1 She said _____ instead of _____ .

2 He said _____ instead of _____ .

3 She said _____ instead of _____ .

C **PAIR WORK** Choose one of the machines above, and give instructions on how to use it. Add any additional instructions.

"To use a record player, first plug it in. Then…"

3 Speaking Step-by-step

A **PAIR WORK** Choose a topic from the list below or your own idea. Make a list of instructions about how to do it.

| attach a file to an email |
| stream movies on a smartphone |
| create a playlist |
| download a podcast |
| make an international call |
| send a text message |
| upload a video |

How to _____
1.
2.
3.
4.
5.

B **PAIR WORK** Give your instructions to another classmate. Answer any questions.

A: *To attach a file to an email, first open your email account. After that, click "compose." Next, …*

I can give instructions. ✓

C Music and me

1 Vocabulary Verb and noun formation

A 🎧 Match the phrases and the pictures. Then listen and check your answers.

a	**announce** a tour	c	**compose** music	e	**perform** a song	g	**record** a song
b	**appreciate** music	d	**entertain** an audience	f	**produce** a song	h	**release** a new album

 1 ☐

 2 ☐

 3 ☐

 4 ☐

 5 ☐

 6 ☐

 7 ☐

 8 ☐

B 🎧 Write the noun forms of the verbs in Part A. Then listen and check your answers.

a   <u>announcement</u>   c _____   e _____   g _____

b _____   d _____   f _____   h _____

C **PAIR WORK** Do you know any friends, artists, or other people who do or have done the things in Part A? Tell your partner.

2 Conversation I'm his biggest fan!

A 🎧 Listen to the conversation. What does Andy tell Miranda to listen to?

Andy	Oh, look! Richie Starr is going to perform here.
Miranda	Yeah, I know. I'm planning to go.
Andy	Really? Have you gotten a ticket yet?
Miranda	Not yet. But I think you can still get them. I didn't know you were a fan.
Andy	Are you kidding? I'm his biggest fan!
Miranda	Have you heard his new album?
Andy	He hasn't released it yet. But I've already downloaded his new single. Here, listen.
Miranda	Nice! I hear he has a cool online fan club.
Andy	He does. It gives information about new album releases and announces all upcoming performances.

B 🎧 Listen to the rest of the conversation. Why didn't Andy know about the concert?

108

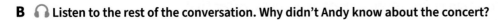

3 Grammar 🎧 Present perfect with *yet* and *already*

In questions, use yet *when you expect the action to have happened.* **Have** you **gotten** a ticket **yet?** **Has** he **released** his album **yet?**	*In responses,* already *means the action has happened earlier.* Yes, I**'ve already gotten** a ticket. Yes, he**'s already released** it.	*In responses,* yet *means the action hasn't happened, but you expect it to.* No, I **haven't gotten** a ticket **yet.** No, **not yet.** He **hasn't released** it **yet.**

A Write sentences in the present perfect with *already* and *yet* about a musician's goals. Then compare with a partner.

1 He has already written four new songs.
2 _____
3 _____
4 _____ -
5 _____
6 _____

My Music Goals

- ☑ write four new songs
- ☐ record two songs for his album
- ☐ release his new album
- ☑ entertain children at the hospital
- ☑ give a free performance in the park
- ☐ announce his retirement

B **PAIR WORK** Look at the musician's answers in Part A. Ask questions with *yet* and answer them.

4 Pronunciation Syllable stress

A 🎧 Listen and repeat. Notice how the stress stays on the same syllable when these verbs become nouns.

an**nounce**	enter**tain**	per**form**	pro**duce**
an**nounce**ment	enter**tain**ment	per**form**ance	pro**duc**tion

B 🎧 Listen. Circle the verb-noun pairs if the stress stays the same.

appreciate	compose	record	release
appreciation	composition	recording	release

5 Speaking The latest

A **CLASS ACTIVITY** Complete the questions with your own ideas. Then find someone who has already done each thing, and ask questions for more information.

- Have you heard _____ (a new album or song) yet?
- Have you played _____ (a new video game) yet?
- Have you seen _____ (a new TV show or movie) yet?
- _____?

B **GROUP WORK** Share your information.

6 Keep talking!

Student A go to page 147 and Student B go to page 148 for more practice.

I can talk about things I've done recently. ☑

D Making your own music

1 Reading 🎧

A What are music streaming sites? What sites do you listen to?

B Read the guide. Why do musicians have to market their music?

A Guide To Breaking Into The Music Business

In the past, successful music acts were supported by record labels that marketed and promoted their music. Although very few artists got high-priced recording contracts, it gave the artists a better chance to become well-known if they got "signed." Today, however, musicians all over the world are creating and recording their own music, and marketing it to fans without the help of record companies. Artists like Chance the Rapper, Glass Animals, and Anne-Marie have succeeded by making their music available to fans through streaming websites.

Here's how to take your self-made music directly to fans.

1. **Record.** If you haven't recorded something yet, you'll need to produce at least one great-sounding song and a music video to go with it.

2. **Upload.** Create a website where fans can download your music and find out how to follow you. You should also upload your music to streaming sites like Bandcamp, where music lovers go to discover new artists and bands.

3. **Market.** Go social. Try to gain followers on popular social media sites like Facebook, Twitter, Instagram, and Snapchat, and promote your music there. Don't forget to include links to your website.

4. **Track.** When someone wants to view, buy or download your song, be sure to have them like your site, follow you on Twitter or get their email address first. Then you can send them news and information about new releases and performances.

5. **Connect.** Use email, blogs, and social media to communicate with fans, giving them a personal connection to you, the artist.

Of course, now that anyone can take their music directly to fans, there is a lot more competition. Only a very few artists become rich and famous this way, but direct-to-fan marketing can help you find an audience that will appreciate your music.

C Read the guide again. Answer the questions.

1 In the past, how did artists become successful and well-known?

2 Where can artists promote their music now?

3 Why should musicians get email addresses of fans?

4 What does a musician need to do before marketing a song?

5 How do artists communicate with fans?

D PAIR WORK What kind of music do you like? How do you discover new music, artists and bands?

2 **Writing** A music review

A Write a review of an album (or a song) you'd recommend. Use the questions and the model to help you.

- What's the name of the album / song?
- When was it released?
- What do you like about the album / song?
- Is there anything you don't like about it?
- Why would you recommend it?

B CLASS ACTIVITY Post your reviews around the room. Read your classmates' reviews. Which songs or albums have you heard?

Momento

Bebel Gilberto's album Momento *was released in 2007. All of the songs are good, but the title song is excellent. On the album, she blends Brazilian bossa nova with electronica and has a beautiful-sounding voice. The only thing I don't like about it is that there aren't enough songs! I'd recommend it because it was recorded with Japanese guitarist Masa Shimizu and . . .*

3 **Listening** Song dedications

A 🎧 Listen to five people call a radio show to dedicate songs to family members. Who do they dedicate songs to? Write the people in the chart.

	People	Song titles
1	friend	
2		
3		
4		
5		

B 🎧 Listen again. What are the song titles? Complete the chart.

C PAIR WORK Imagine you can dedicate a song to someone. What song would you dedicate and to whom? Why? Tell your partner.

4 **Speaking** Soundtrack of my life

A Make a list of three songs that remind you of particular times or events in your life.

	Song titles	Memories
1		
2		
3		

B GROUP WORK Discuss your songs and memories. Ask and answer questions for more information.

A: The song . . . reminds me of middle school. It was my favorite song when I was 14.

B: I know that song! How *do* you feel now when you hear it?

A: Oh, I feel totally embarrassed. I can't stand it now!

Wrap-up

1 Quick pair review

Lesson A `Brainstorm!`

Make a list of words and phrases related to music. How many do you know?
You have two minutes.

Lesson B `Do you remember?`

Complete the sentences with words or phrases to give instructions. You have
one minute.

How to install software:

_____ find the software on its official website.

_____ download and click "install."

_____ restart your computer.

How to get money out of an ATM:

_____ put your ATM card in the machine.

_____ type in your code.

_____ select how much money you want.

Lesson C `Find out!`

What are two things both you and your partner have already done today?
What are two things you both haven't done yet? You have three minutes.

Lesson D `Test your partner!`

Say (or sing) the words to a song you know in English. Can your partner guess
the title and singer? You have two minutes.

2 In the real world

Who is your favorite singer? Go to the singer's website, and find information
about his or her albums. Then write about them.

- What was the singer's first album? When was it released?
- When was the singer's last album released? Did it have any hit songs?
- What's your favorite song by this singer? What's it about?

Taylor Swift

My favorite singer is Taylor Swift. Her first album was
called *Taylor Swift*. It was released in 2006. I love it. My
favorite song on the album is called "Tim McGraw," who is
a famous country music singer himself. Taylor was only
sixteen years old when the song was released. The song
is about how one of Tim McGraw's songs always reminds
her of . . .

12 On vacation

Lesson A

- Vacation activities
- Gerunds

Lesson B

- Asking about preferences
- Reminding someone of something

Lesson C

- Extreme sports
- Modals for necessity and recommendations

Lesson D

- Reading "A Taste of Cairo"
- Writing: A walking tour

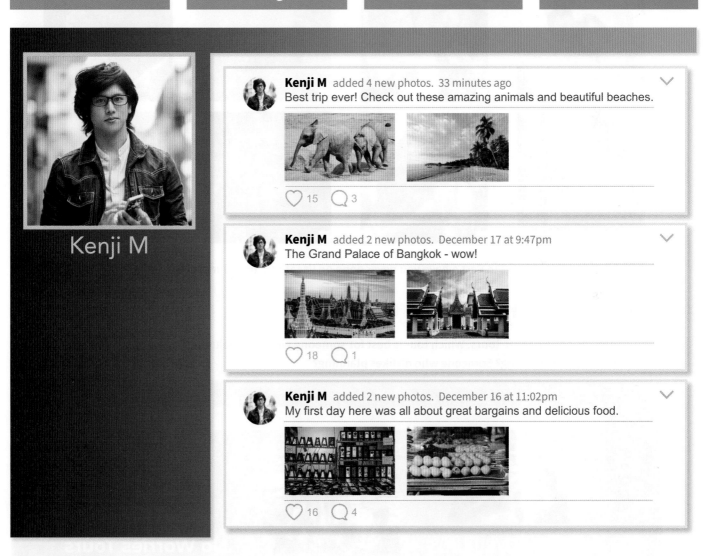

Kenji M

Kenji M added 4 new photos. 33 minutes ago
Best trip ever! Check out these amazing animals and beautiful beaches.

♡ 15   💬 3

Kenji M added 2 new photos. December 17 at 9:47pm
The Grand Palace of Bangkok - wow!

♡ 18   💬 1

Kenji M added 2 new photos. December 16 at 11:02pm
My first day here was all about great bargains and delicious food.

♡ 16   💬 4

Warm Up

A Look at Kenji's social media posts. Where did he go on his vacation? What do you think he did there?

B What do you like to do on vacation? What kinds of things do you usually bring back with you?

A Travel preferences

1 Vocabulary Vacation activities

A 🎧 Match the phrases and the pictures. Then listen and check your answers.

a	buy handicrafts	c	listen to live music	e	speak a foreign language	g	visit landmarks
b	go to clubs	d	see wildlife	f	try local food	h	volunteer

 1 ☐

 2 ☐

 3 ☐

 4 ☐

 5 ☐

 6 ☐

 7 ☐

 8 ☐

B **PAIR WORK** Which things in Part A have you *never* done on vacation? Tell your partner.

2 Language in context Three types of tours

A 🎧 Read the ads for three tours. Which tour is best for someone who likes volunteering? Someone who likes eating? Someone who dislikes planning?

80%   4:21PM

Cuisine Adventures
Trying local foods is a great way to learn about a culture. Call today if you are interested in joining our "Eat and Learn" tour.

ENVIRONMENTAL EXPERIENCES
Are you concerned about protecting the environment? Volunteering is a rewarding way to spend a vacation. Choose from over 20 tours.

No Worries Tours
Do you enjoy traveling by bus but dislike planning the details? We specialize in organizing tours with no stress.

B What about you? Which tour interests you? Why?

3 Grammar ♫ Gerunds

A gerund is an –ing word that acts like a noun. Gerunds may be the subject of a sentence, or they may appear after some verbs or prepositions.

As subjects:	**Trying** local foods is a great way to learn about a culture.
	Volunteering is a rewarding way to spend a vacation.
After some verbs:	I **enjoy traveling** by bus.
	I **dislike planning** the travel details.
After prepositions:	I'm interested **in joining** the "Eat and Learn" tour.
	I'm concerned **about protecting** the environment.

A Complete the conversations with the gerund forms of the verbs. Then compare with a partner.

be	buy	get	go	help	lose	meet	✓travel	try	volunteer

1 **A** Do you enjoy _____traveling_____ alone or in a group?

  B I prefer _____ in a large group. It's more fun.

2 **A** Are you interested in _____ handicrafts when you travel?

  B Not really. I like _____ to markets, but just to look.

3 **A** _____ local food is the best way to learn about a culture. Don't you agree?

  B I'm not really sure. _____ local people is also good.

4 **A** Are you worried about _____ sick when you travel abroad?

  B Not really. I'm more concerned about _____ my passport!

5 **A** Do you think _____ on vacation would be fun?

  B I do. _____ other people is a great thing to do.

B **PAIR WORK** Ask and answer the questions in Part A. Answer with your own information.

4 Speaking Travel talk

A Complete the questions with your own ideas. Use gerunds.

- Do you enjoy _____ when you're on vacation?
- Are you interested in _____ on vacation?
- Which is more interesting on vacation, _____ or _____ ?
- Are you ever concerned about _____ when you travel?
- As a tourist, is _____ important to you?
- _____ ?
- _____ ?

B **GROUP WORK** Discuss your questions. Ask and answer questions to get more information.

5 Keep talking!

Go to page 149 for more practice.

I can discuss travel preferences. ✓

B Don't forget to . . .

1 Interactions Preferences and reminders

A Where do you usually stay when you travel? A hotel? A youth hostel?

B 🎧 Listen to the conversation. What doesn't the guest need help with? Then practice the conversation.

Clerk	Can I help you?
Guest	Yes. I'm looking for a room for two nights.
Clerk	Do you have a reservation?
Guest	No, I don't.
Clerk	Let me see what we have. Would you like a single room or a double room?
Guest	A single is fine. I only need one bed.
Clerk	I can give you room 13A. Please sign here. And there's a free breakfast from 7:00 to 9:00.
Guest	Oh, great. Thank you very much.
Clerk	Here's your key. Do you need help with your bag?
Guest	No, that's all right.
Clerk	OK. Remember to leave your key at the front desk when you go out.
Guest	No problem.
Clerk	Enjoy your stay.

C 🎧 Read the expressions below. Complete each box with a similar expression from the conversation. Then listen and check your answers.

Asking about preferences	**Reminding someone of something**
_____	_____
(Would you prefer . . . or . . . ?)	(Don't forget to . . .)
(Would you rather have . . . or . . . ?)	(Let me remind you to . . .)

D Match the sentences and the responses. Then practice with a partner.

1 May I help you? _____
2 Would you like a single room? _____
3 Would you prefer a garden or an ocean view? _____
4 Please remember to lock your door at night. _____
5 Don't forget to check out by 11:00. _____

a. I don't know. Which one is cheaper?
b. Eleven? I thought it was by noon.
c. Actually, we need a double.
d. Yes. I have a reservation for one night.
e. I will. Thanks for the reminder.

2 Listening At a hostel

A 🎧 Listen to a backpacker check into a hostel. Complete the form with the correct information.

Sydney Backpackers

Type of room:

☐ single   ☐ double   ☐ triple   ☐ dorm

Number of nights? _____

Bathroom? ☐ yes ☐ no   **Breakfast?** ☐ yes ☐ no

Method of payment:

☐ cash   ☐ credit card

Room number: _____

B 🎧 Listen again. Answer the questions.

1 Why doesn't she get a single room? _____

2 What time is breakfast? _____

3 What floor is her room on? _____

4 What does the receptionist remind her to do? _____

3 Speaking Role play

PAIR WORK Role-play the situation. Then change roles.

Student A: You want a room at a hotel. Student B is the clerk at the front desk. Circle your preferences. Then check in.

- You want a **single** / **double** room.
- You want to stay for **two** / **three** / **four** nights.
- You **want** / **don't want** your own bathroom.
- You **want** / **don't want** breakfast.

Student B: You are the clerk at the front desk of a hotel. Check Student A in. At the end, remind him or her of something.

B: Can I help you?

A: Yes, thank you. I'd like a room, please.

B: All right. Would you prefer a single or a double?

A: I'd prefer . . .

B: How many nights would you like to stay?

A: . . .

B: . . . And please don't forget . . .

I can ask about preferences. ☑

I can remind someone of something. ☑

C Rules and recommendations

1 Vocabulary Extreme sports

A 🎧 **Label the pictures with the correct words. Then listen and check your answers.**

bungee jumping	paragliding	skydiving	waterskiing
kite surfing	rock climbing	snowboarding	white-water rafting

1 _____

2 _____

3 _____

4 _____

5 _____

6 _____

7 _____

8 _____

B **PAIR WORK** **Which sports would you consider trying? Which wouldn't you do? Why not? Tell your partner.**

2 Conversation First-time snowboarder

A 🎧 **Listen to the conversation. Why does Sarah tell Kyle to stay in the beginners' section?**

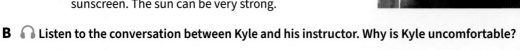

Kyle   Hi. I'd like to rent a snowboard, please.

Sarah   OK. Have you ever been snowboarding?

Kyle   Um, no. But I've skied before.

Sarah   Well, we offer lessons. You don't have to take them, but it's a good idea. You'll learn the basics.

Kyle   All right. When is your next lesson?

Sarah   At 11:00. You've got to complete this form here to sign up.

Kyle   No problem. What else do I need to know?

Sarah   After your lesson, you should stay in the beginners' section for a while. It's safer for the other snowboarders.

Kyle   OK. Anything else?

Sarah   Yes. You must wear a helmet. Oh, and you ought to wear sunscreen. The sun can be very strong.

B 🎧 **Listen to the conversation between Kyle and his instructor. Why is Kyle uncomfortable?**

3 Grammar 🎧 Modals for necessity and recommendations

Necessity
You **must** wear a helmet.
You**'ve got to** complete this form.
You **have to** listen to your instructor.
Lack of necessity
You **don't have to** take a lesson.

Recommendations
You**'d better** be back before dark.
You **ought to** wear sunscreen.
You **should** stay in the beginners' section.
You **shouldn't** go in the advanced section.

A Circle the best travel advice. Then compare with a partner.

1 You **should / must** get a passport before you go abroad. Everybody needs one.

2 You **don't have to / 've got to** visit every landmark. Choose just a few instead.

3 You **should / don't have to** book a hotel online. It's often cheaper that way.

4 You **ought to / shouldn't** get to your hotel too early. You can't check in until 2:00.

5 You **shouldn't / 'd better** keep your money in a safe place. Losing it would be awful.

6 You **have to / should** pay for some things in cash. Many places don't take credit cards.

7 You **must / don't have to** show your student ID to get a discount. Don't forget it!

8 You **ought to / shouldn't** try some local food. It can be full of nice surprises!

B **PAIR WORK** What advice would you give? Complete the sentences with modals for necessity or recommendations. Then compare answers.

1 You _____ go paragliding on a very windy day.

2 You _____ have experience to go waterskiing.

3 You _____ have special equipment to go bungee jumping.

4 You _____ be in good shape to go kite surfing.

4 Pronunciation Reduction of verbs

A 🎧 Listen and repeat. Notice the reduction of the modal verbs.

You**'ve got to** pay in cash.   You **have to** check out by noon.   You **ought to** try the food.

B **PAIR WORK** Practice the sentences in Exercise 3. Reduce the modal verbs.

5 Speaking Rules of the game

A **GROUP WORK** Choose an extreme sport from Exercise 1. What rules do you think there are? What recommendations would you give to someone who wanted to try it?

A: You must sign a form before you go bungee jumping.

B: Yeah. And you should wear a helmet.

C: Oh, and you shouldn't be afraid.

B **CLASS ACTIVITY** Share your ideas.

6 Keep talking!

Go to page 150 for more practice.

I can talk about rules and recommendations. ✓

D Seeing the sights

1 Reading 🎧

A Do you ever read food or travel blogs? Do you ever watch food or travel TV shows?

B Read the blog. Write the headings above the correct paragraphs.

> A Delicious Dinner   Juice Break   The Market   Sweet Shop

Home   About Arlen   My Blog   Q&A   Messages   Video   Recipes

A TASTE OF CAIRO

Cookbook author Arlen Gargagliano is always looking for new travel experiences. Join her on her blog as she takes a food tour of Cairo, Egypt.

_____ 1:45 p.m.

Today I walked through the narrow streets of a famous Cairo market. There were many areas to explore, but my favorite was the spice market. Each shop had huge containers of colorful spices. I bought a bag of mixed spices for a friend and some dark henna to dye my hair red!

_____ 3:15 p.m.

I stopped for one of my favorite drinks – sugar cane juice! A man took pieces of sugar cane, put them in a machine, and made juice. He gave me a glass of the juice, and I drank it quickly. It was sweet and delicious! It gave me lots of energy.

_____ 6:30 p.m.

I ate dinner at the Abou el Sid restaurant. I tried several appetizers. My two favorites were a creamy bean dish in a spicy sauce and fried eggplant with garlic. I had them with fresh flatbread. I also tried a famous Egyptian dish made with a green vegetable. I want to live in this place!

_____ 8:00 p.m.

Before walking back to the hotel, I made one last stop at a place that sells wonderful Egyptian sweets in el Hussein Square. It was busy, but I sat down and ordered a cup of tea and _basbousa_, a kind of cake made with semolina and sugar syrup. It was out of this world!

C Read the blog again. Write the initials of the blog headings (D, J, M, or S) in which Arlen did the activities below. (More than one answer is possible.)

1 ate a meal _____   3 drank something _____   5 saw spices _____

2 bought a gift _____   4 had something sweet _____   6 tried vegetables _____

D **PAIR WORK** Would you enjoy a tour like this? Why or why not? Discuss your ideas.

2 **Writing** A walking tour

A PAIR WORK **Choose a topic for an interesting walking tour in your town or city. Use one of the topics below or your own idea.**

architecture and design	historical sights	parks and nature
food and drink	nightlife	shopping

B PAIR WORK **Write a description of your walking tour.**

Historic Old San Juan

To really learn about the history of Puerto Rico, you have to walk through Old San Juan. You should start your walking tour at the city walls. Follow these walls along the sea to San Juan Gate, which was built around 1635. Go through the gate, turn right, and walk uphill. At the end of the street you can see La Fortaleza . . .

La Fortaleza
Old San Juan, Puerto Rico

C GROUP WORK **Present your tour to another pair. Did you include any of the same places?**

3 **Listening** An adventure tour

A 🎧 **Listen to a guide talk to some tourists before a Grand Canyon rafting trip. What does the guide tell the tourists to do? Check (✓) the correct answers.**

- ☐ wear a safety vest
- ☐ wear sunscreen
- ☐ bring your cell phone
- ☐ drink a lot of water
- ☐ wear a hat
- ☐ wear a swimsuit
- ☐ bring water
- ☐ leave your camera
- ☐ wear tennis shoes
- ☐ bring food
- ☐ bring plastic bags
- ☐ listen to your guide

B 🎧 **Listen again. Are the statements true or false? Write T (true) or F (false).**

1   The most important thing to remember is to have fun. _____

2   The tourists need to wear safety vests at all times on the raft. _____

3   There is no eating or drinking allowed. _____

4   The tourists shouldn't leave their phones on the bus. _____

4 **Speaking** Dream trip

A **Imagine you can go anywhere in the world for three weeks. Answer the questions.**

- What kind of trip are you interested in taking?
- What places would you like to visit? Why?
- What would you like to do in each place?
- How long do you plan to spend in each place?
- How can you get from place to place?

B PAIR WORK **Tell your partner about your dream trip. Ask and answer questions for more information.**

I can describe my dream trip. ✓

Wrap-up

1 Quick pair review

Lesson A `Test your partner!`

Say four vacation activities. Can your partner use the gerund form of the phrase in a sentence correctly? You have three minutes.

A: *See wildlife.*

B: *I'm not interested in seeing wildlife on vacation.*

Lesson B `Give your opinion!`

Ask your partner which vacation he or she prefers from each pair of pictures. Then remind your partner to do or take something on the trip. Take turns. You have two minutes.

A: Would you prefer going to an island or to the mountains?

B: I'd prefer going to an island.

A: OK. Remember to take sunscreen.

Lesson C `Brainstorm!`

Make a list of extreme sports people do in the water, in the air, and on land. How many do you know? You have one minute.

Lesson D `Guess!`

Describe your dream trip to your partner, but don't say where it is. Can your partner guess where it is? Take turns. You have two minutes.

2 In the real world

Go online and find recommendations in English for people who want to try a new sport. Use one of the sports below or your own idea. Then write about it.

sandboarding	downhill mountain biking	base jumping	bodyboarding

Sandboarding

Sandboarding is like snowboarding, but you do it on sand, not snow. You must have a sandboard for this sport. You should wear glasses so that you don't get sand in your eyes.

Left brain / right brain

A **PAIR WORK** Interview your partner. Check (✓) his or her answers.

Left Brain vs. Right Brain

Do you use your right or left brain more often? Try this fun quiz and find out.

1 How do you remember things?
- [ ] a. with words
- [ ] b. with pictures
- [ ] c. both

2 Which can you remember easily?
- [ ] a. names
- [ ] b. faces
- [ ] c. both

3 Which math subject do you like?
- [ ] a. algebra
- [ ] b. geometry
- [ ] c. both

4 How do you like to work in class?
- [ ] a. alone
- [ ] b. in groups
- [ ] c. both

5 How do you like to study alone?
- [ ] a. quietly
- [ ] b. with music playing
- [ ] c. both

6 Which activity do you enjoy?
- [ ] a. writing
- [ ] b. drawing
- [ ] c. both

7 What kinds of tests do you like?
- [ ] a. multiple choice
- [ ] b. essay
- [ ] c. both

8 How do you like things explained to you?
- [ ] a. with words
- [ ] b. with actions
- [ ] c. both

9 What do you use to make decisions?
- [ ] a. the facts
- [ ] b. my experience
- [ ] c. both

10 How do you like to solve problems?
- [ ] a. one at a time
- [ ] b. at the same time
- [ ] c. both

11 How do you manage your time?
- [ ] a. very carefully
- [ ] b. not very carefully
- [ ] c. both

12 Which animals do you like?
- [ ] a. dogs
- [ ] b. cats
- [ ] c. both

Source: library.thinkquest.org

B **PAIR WORK** Score your partner's answers. Is he or she left-brained or right-brained? (More *c* answers or the same number of *a* and *b* answers means your partner has traits for both.)

More *a* answers: Left-brained	More *b* answers: Right-brained
More verbal than visual	More visual than verbal
Likes to do things step by step	Likes to do things at the same time
Very organized	Not always organized
Follows rules without questioning	Often asks why
Strong sense of time	Little sense of time
Learns by seeing	Learns by doing
Uses few gestures when talking	Talks with hands
Listens to what is said	Listens to how something is said

C **GROUP WORK** Do your results in Part B describe you well? What do you think your results say about your personality?

People on my mind

A Write the name of someone you know for each description. Then think about answers to the questions.

Someone I miss very much:

_____

● How long have you known this person?
● When did you last see him or her?
● When will you see each other again?

Someone who gave me a special gift:

_____

● What was the gift?
● How long have you had it?
● What made the gift special?

Someone I'd like to know better:

_____

● How long have you known this person?
● When was the last time you spoke?
● What's he or she like?

Someone I've admired since I was a child:

_____

● When did you first meet this person?
● What do you admire about him or her?
● Do you share any of the same qualities?

B **PAIR WORK** Interview your partner about each person. Ask questions for more information.

A: Who is someone you miss very much?

B: I miss my grandmother very much.

A: How long have you known her?

B: I've known her since I was born! But I haven't seen her since April.

Keep talking!

A green quiz

A **PAIR WORK** Interview your partner. Circle his or her answers.

HOW GREEN ARE YOU?
Try this quiz to find out.

1 You're leaving for the weekend, but you're not taking your computer. What do you do?
a. Put it to "sleep."
b. Shut it down.
c. Turn it off and unplug it.

2 You're planning to go to a movie with several friends. What do you do?
a. Go in separate cars.
b. Meet and go in one car.
c. Take public transportation.

3 You're walking and you see some empty bottles on the sidewalk. What do you do?
a. Leave the bottles there.
b. Put them in a garbage can.
c. Put them in a recycling bin.

4 Your school has water fountains for people to drink from. What do you do?
a. Buy bottled water instead.
b. Drink directly from the water fountains.
c. Fill up your own water bottle.

5 You're buying a magazine, and the cashier starts to put it in a bag. What do you do?
a. Take the bag and throw it away later.
b. Take the bag, but reuse it.
c. Just take the magazine.

6 You have some old, unused medicine that you don't need. What do you do?
a. Flush it down the toilet.
b. Throw it in the garbage.
c. Return it to a pharmacy.

7 You're making a salad and realize you don't have enough lettuce. What do you do?
a. Get any lettuce at the nearest store.
b. Buy organic lettuce at a farmer's market.
c. Pick some lettuce from your own garden.

8 A company in your neighborhood is harming the environment. What do you do?
a. Nothing.
b. Tell your friends.
c. Write a letter to the local newspaper about it.

B **PAIR WORK** Score your partner's answers. How green is he or she? Are the results accurate?

a answers = 0 points	11—16 Congratulations! You lead a very green life.
b answers = 1 point	6—10 You're green in some ways, but not in others.
c answers = 2 points	0—5 You're not very green. It's not too late to change!

C **PAIR WORK** What other things do you do to help the environment? Tell your partner.

Be an optimist!

A **PAIR WORK** Add two situations to the chart. Then discuss what will, could, or might happen in each situation. Take notes.

If we . . . ,	we will . . .	we might . . .
eat too much fast food		
spend all day at the beach		
use cell phones in class		
read the news every day		
never study English		
watch too much TV		
don't get enough sleep		
spend too much time online		

A: What do you think will happen if we eat too much fast food?

B: If we eat too much fast food, we'll gain weight.

B **GROUP WORK** Share your ideas with another pair. Which ideas are the best? Do you have any other ideas?

Keep talking!

What to do?

A GROUP WORK Imagine you have one of the relationship problems below. Your group gives you advice. Take turns.

My friend texts me constantly and then gets angry if I don't answer right away. Is it important to answer every text? I'm not sure what to do about this. I prefer to communicate by phone.

My sister has a new hairstyle, and I think it looks pretty awful. I don't really want to criticize her, but I think it's a good idea to say something to her. But what exactly do I say?

My co-worker won't talk to me. She says I gossiped about her. I guess I did, but it wasn't anything serious. It feels like she's judging me. I hope she can forgive me. After all, we need to work together.

My classmate always tries to copy my answers when we are taking tests or working on our own. It makes me angry. I don't want the teacher to think I'm cheating, too. Should I tell my teacher?

A: My friend texts me constantly and then . . .

B: It's not important to answer every text. Just ignore them.

C: But it's not good to ignore them. Say something to your friend about it.

D: That's good advice. It's also a good idea to . . .

B GROUP WORK Which advice was the best? Why? Tell your group.

"Maria gave the best advice. It's important to tell the truth."

C GROUP WORK Have you ever given relationship advice to someone? Who? What was the advice? Tell your group.

Keep talking!

What do you think?

A PAIR WORK Look at the picture. Make one speculation about each person. Use *must*, *could*, *can't*, *may*, or *might*.

Keep talking!

A: Diego is buying a dress, but it can't be for his wife. It's too small.

B: Right. He might be buying it for his daughter.

A: Yeah. And he must be rich. The store looks very expensive.

B GROUP WORK Compare your speculations with another pair. Did you make any of the same ones?

Keep talking!

Reflections

A **CLASS ACTIVITY** Find classmates who answer "yes" to each question. Write their names and ask questions for more information.

Questions	Name	Extra information
1 Have you ever eaten an entire pizza by yourself?		
2 Do you learn better by studying in a group than by yourself?		
3 Did you teach yourself how to cook?		
4 Do you see yourself living in another country in five years?		
5 Have you ever traveled anywhere by yourself?		
6 Would you like to change something about yourself?		
7 Have you ever lived by yourself?		
8 Do you know someone who taught himself or herself a foreign language?		

A: Have you ever eaten an entire pizza by yourself?

B: Yes, I have!

A: Wow! That's a lot of pizza. What kind of pizza was it?

B: It had cheese, pepperoni, onions, and peppers on it.

B Share your information. What's the most interesting thing you learned? Who else in the class answered "yes" to each question?

Keep talking!

Imagine that!

A Guess your partner's answers to the questions. Write your guesses in the chart.

Questions	My guesses	My partner's answers
1 What would you do if you saw your favorite celebrity?		
2 What would you do if your best friend moved to another country?		
3 How would you feel if someone brought up something embarrassing about you at a party?		
4 What would you do if you broke something expensive in a store?		
5 Where would you go if you had one week to travel anywhere in the world?		
6 What would you do if a friend borrowed some money from you and then didn't pay you back?		
7 What would you do if your grades in this class suddenly dropped?		

B **PAIR WORK** Interview your partner. Complete the chart with his or her answers. How many of your partner's answers did you guess correctly?

C **CLASS ACTIVITY** Do any of your partner's answers surprise you? Would you and your partner do any similar things? Tell the class.

Keep talking!

Facts and opinions

A GROUP WORK Add two sets of questions about music to the list. Then discuss the questions. Ask follow-up questions to get more information.

1 What bands were formed in the 1960s? '70s? '80s? '90s? What was their music like?

2 What male singer do you think has a nice-sounding voice? What female singer?

3 What well-known singers or bands do you not like very much? Why not?

4 Were any record-breaking hits released last year? What did you think of the songs?

5 Was any truly awful music released in the past few years? What made it so terrible?

6 What was the last music awards show you saw on TV? Who was on it?

7 Who are the best-selling singers from your country? Do you enjoy their music?

8 What are some easily learned songs in your native language? Do you know all the words?

9 _____ ? _____ ?

10 _____ ? _____ ?

The Rolling Stones, 1960s

ABBA, 1970s

R.E.M., 1980s

The Spice Girls, 1990s

A: The Rolling Stones were formed in the 1960s.

B: How was their music?

A: Their music was fantastic. It still is.

C: Can you name the band members?

B CLASS ACTIVITY Share any interesting information.

Keep talking!

Find the differences

Student A

You and your partner have pictures of Monica and Victor, but they aren't exactly the same.
Ask questions with *yet* to find the differences. Circle the items that are different.

see a movie

get a new TV

download a song

send a text

buy a video game

sing a song

A: Have Monica and Victor seen a movie yet?

B: No, they haven't. In my picture, they haven't seen it yet. They're going inside.

A: So that's different. In my picture, they're leaving the movie theater.

Keep talking! 147

Find the differences

Student B

You and your partner have pictures of Monica and Victor, but they aren't exactly the same. Ask questions with *yet* to find the differences. Circle the items that are different.

see a movie

get a new TV

download a song

send a text

buy a video game

sing a song

A: Have Monica and Victor seen a movie yet?

B: No, they haven't. In my picture, they haven't seen it yet. They're going inside.

A: So that's different. In my picture, they're leaving the movie theater.

Keep talking!

Travel partners

A Add three questions about travel preferences to the chart. Then check (✓) your answers.

When you travel, . . .	Me		Name: _____	
	Yes	No	Yes	No
1 do you like being in a large group?	☐	☐	☐	☐
2 are you interested in meeting new people?	☐	☐	☐	☐
3 is saving money important to you?	☐	☐	☐	☐
4 do you like trying new foods?	☐	☐	☐	☐
5 is asking directions embarrassing to you?	☐	☐	☐	☐
6 do you like knowing your schedule in advance?	☐	☐	☐	☐
7 is camping more fun than staying in hotels?	☐	☐	☐	☐
8 do you enjoy shopping for souvenirs?	☐	☐	☐	☐
9 do you like big cities?	☐	☐	☐	☐
10 do you like going to clubs?	☐	☐	☐	☐
11 is seeing everything possible important to you?	☐	☐	☐	☐
12	☐	☐	☐	☐
13	☐	☐	☐	☐
14	☐	☐	☐	☐

B PAIR WORK Interview your partner. Complete the chart with his or her answers.

C PAIR WORK Compare your answers. Would you make good travel partners? Why or why not?

A: We wouldn't make good travel partners. You like being in a large group. I don't.

B: Yes, but we're both interested in meeting new people.

A: Well, that's true. And saving money is important to us.

Keep talking! 149

A backpacking trip

A PAIR WORK Imagine someone is planning a two-week backpacking trip to your country. What rules and recommendations would you give for each category? Take notes.

Packing	Communication
Health and safety	Places to stay
Transportation	Money
Food	Other

 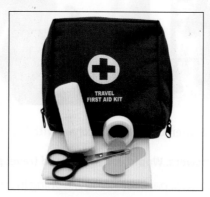 

B GROUP WORK Share your ideas with another pair. Did you have any of the same rules or recommendations? Can you think of any other rules or recommendations?

A: You shouldn't pack too many clothes.

B: Yes, but you have to have enough clothes!

C: Also, you ought to bring your cell phone.

Keep talking!

Irregular verbs

Base form	Simple past	Past participle
be	was, were	been
become	became	become
break	broke	broken
build	built	built
buy	bought	bought
choose	chose	chosen
come	came	come
do	did	done
draw	drew	drawn
drink	drank	drunk
drive	drove	driven
eat	ate	eaten
fall	fell	fallen
feel	felt	felt
fly	flew	flown
forget	forgot	forgotten
get	got	gotten
give	gave	given
go	went	gone
hang	hung	hung
have	had	had
hear	heard	heard
hold	held	held
know	knew	known
leave	left	left

Base form	Simple past	Past participle
lose	lost	lost
make	made	made
meet	met	met
pay	paid	paid
put	put	put
read	read	read
ride	rode	ridden
run	ran	run
say	said	said
see	saw	seen
sell	sold	sold
send	sent	sent
sing	sang	sung
sit	sat	sat
sleep	slept	slept
speak	spoke	spoken
spend	spent	spent
stand	stood	stood
swim	swam	swum
take	took	taken
teach	taught	taught
think	thought	thought
wear	wore	worn
win	won	won
write	wrote	written

Adjective and adverb formations

Adjectives	Adverbs
agreeable	agreeably
amazing	amazingly
ambitious	ambitiously
angry	angrily
brave	bravely
careful	carefully
confident	confidently
considerate	considerately
creative	creatively
curious	curiously
decisive	decisively
disagreeable	disagreeably
dishonest	dishonestly
early	early
easy	easily
enthusiastic	enthusiastically
extreme	extremely
fair	fairly
fashionable	fashionably
fast	fast
fortunate	fortunately
glamorous	glamorously
good	well
hard	hard
honest	honestly

Adjectives	Adverbs
immature	immaturely
impatient	impatiently
inconsiderate	inconsiderately
indecisive	indecisively
interesting	interestingly
late	late
lucky	luckily
mature	maturely
nervous	nervously
optimistic	optimistically
patient	patiently
quick	quickly
rare	rarely
reliable	reliably
sad	sadly
serious	seriously
similar	similarly
strange	strangely
stubborn	stubbornly
sudden	suddenly
surprising	surprisingly
unfair	unfairly
unfortunate	unfortunately
unreliable	unreliably
wise	wisely

Answer Key

Answer Key

Unit 7 Lesson D (page 71)

Listening

This personality test is just for fun. Don't take the answers *too* seriously!

1 This person is the most important person in your life.
2 If you see a big animal, you think you have big problems.
3 If you have a big house, you are very ambitious.
4 If the door is open, you're happy for people to visit anytime. If it's closed, you prefer people to call first.
5 If there is food or flowers on the table, you are very optimistic.
6 If the material is strong (like metal or plastic), you have a strong relationship with the person in number 1.
7 If you keep the cup, you want to keep a good relationship with the person in number 1.

Credits

The authors and publishers acknowledge the following sources of copyright material and are grateful for the permissions granted. While every effort has been made, it has not always been possible to identify the sources of all the material used, or to trace all copyright holders. If any omissions are brought to our notice, we will be happy to include the appropriate acknowledgements on reprinting and in the next update to the digital edition, as applicable.

Photography

All the photographs are sourced from Getty Images.
U1: Steve Debenport/E+; Hero Images; PeopleImages/DigitalVision; sturti/E+; Kwanchai Lerttanapunyaporn/EyeEm; ArisSu/iStock/Getty Images Plus; bonniej/E+; Tim Hall/Cultura; Lee Pettet/Stockbyte; Ca-ssis/iStock/Getty Images Plus; kali9/E+; studo58/iStock/Getty Images Plus; Peter Zvonar/Moment Open; paylessimages/iStock/Getty Images Plus; Caiaimage/Sam Edwards; James Griffiths Photography/iStock/Getty Images Plus; Simon McGill/Moment; 9wut/iStock/Getty Images Plus; trekandshoot/iStock/Getty Images Plus; Design Pics/Craig Tuttle; Chris Ryan/OJO Images; Rob Lewine; Maksim Kamyshanskii/iStock/Getty Images Plus; winhorse/iStock/Getty Images Plus; JGI/Jamie Grill/Blend Images; Lívia Fernandes - Brazil./Moment; Imgorthand/E+; BONNINSTUDIO/iStock/Getty Images Plus; JGI/Jamie Grill/Tetra images; quavondo/E+; U2: Blend Images - KidStock/Brand X Pictures; Geber86/E+; KatarzynaBialasiewicz/iStock/Getty Images Plus; PeopleImages/E+; Eric Audras/ONOKY; Tetra Images; groveb/iStock/Getty Images Plus; KiraVolkov/iStock/Getty Images Plus; Paul Bradbury/OJO Images; tazytaz/E+; Caiaimage/Tom Merton; Peter Dazeley/Photographer's Choice; Buena Vista Images/DigitalVision; PeopleImages/DigitalVision; George Doyle/Stockbyte; Lew Robertson/Corbis; ©David J Spurdens; Fuse; Juanmonino/E+; Jupiterimages/The Image Bank; NicolasMcComber/E+; cirano83/iStock/Getty Images Plus; Peter Dazeley/Photographer's Choice; MASSIVE/Stone; Image Source/DigitalVision; Peter Dazeley/Photographer's Choice; U3: Hoxton/Tom Merton; Eamonn McCormack/BFC/Getty Images Entertainment; Viktorcvetkovic/E+; Lorado/E+; castillodominici/iStock/Getty Images Plus; Peter Dazeley/Photographer's Choice; Trinette Reed; Tvi Nguyen/EyeEm; Chauncey James/EyeEm; Dirk Saeger/EyeEm; CraigRJD/iStock/Getty Images Plus; Yagi Studio/DigitalVision; Nemia Walter/EyeEm; Phil Boorman/Cultura; Christophel Fine Art/UIG via Getty Images; The Art Collector/Print Collector; Brandon Colbert Photography/Moment; istanbulimage/E+; yasinguneysu/iStock/Getty Images Plus; ksevgi/iStock/Getty Images Plus; stuartbur/iStock/Getty Images Plus; nortongo/iStock/Getty Images Plus; NAKphotos/iStock/Getty Images Plus; Kay-Paris Fernandes/WireImage; Tetra Images; andresr/E+; Indeed; Mimi Haddon/DigitalVision; Morsa Images/DigitalVision; PeopleImages/E+; photosindia; fotostorm/E+; feedough/iStock/Getty Images Plus; Viktoria Ovcharenko/iStock/Getty Images Plus; FangXiaNuo/E+; Michele Quattrin; mQn Photography/Moment; soleg/iStock/Getty Images Plus; Drazen_/E+; Fabrice LEROUGE/ONOKY; U4: RelaxFoto.de/E+; Graiki/Moment; Alexander Jackson/EyeEm; Hill Street Studios/DigitalVision; gpointstudio/iStock/Getty Images Plus; guruXOOX/iStock/Getty Images Plus; TAGSTOCK1/iStock/Getty Images Plus; kali9/E+; Ivanko_Brnjakovic/iStock/Getty Images Plus; andresr/iStock/Getty Images Plus; Elena KHarchenko/iStock/Getty Images Plus; ONOKY - Fabrice LEROUGE/Brand X Pictures; Martin Harvey/Photolibrary; Georgijevic/E+ perfect loop/iStock/Getty Images Plus; Vitalalp/iStock/Getty Images Plus; Pierre-Yves Babelon/Moment; Carso80/iStock Editorial/Getty Images Plus; massimo colombo/Moment; Stewart Cohen/Blend Images; James Osmond/Photolibrary; kimkole/iStock/Getty Images Plus; PeopleImages/DigitalVision; LWA/Dann Tardif/Blend Images; StockFood; Colin Anderson Productions pty ltd/DigitalVision; Trinette Reed/Blend Images; Ricardo Liberato/Moment; DAVID NUNUK/Science Photo Library; Carlos Fernandez/Moment; U5: dblight/E+; Ibon Bastida/EyeEm; Dan77/iStock/Getty Images Plus; Guillaume CHANSON/Moment; Mark Miller Photos/DigitalVision; Christian Ender/Getty Images News; Patricia Hamilton/Moment; ChandraDhas/iStock; Tina Llorca/EyeEm; QQ7/iStock/Getty Images Plus; Pley/iStock/Getty Images Plus; David Madison/Corbis; Kadshah Nagibe/EyeEm; FrankvandenBergh/iStock/Getty Images Plus; Alexander Spatari/Moment; isitsharp/iStock; JAWOC/AFP; Fuse; Feifei Cui-Paoluzzo/Moment; Santiago Urquijo/Moment; Ivan_off/iStock/Getty Images Plus; Alexander Bennett/EyeEm; Tunach/iStock/Getty Images Plus; grebcha/iStock/Getty Images Plus; G-o-o-d-M-a-n/iStock/Getty Images Plus; Robin Smith/The Image Bank; IndiaPictures/Universal Images Group; JaySi/iStock/Getty Images Plus; Michele Falzone/The Image Bank; Feng Wei Photography/Moment; Torresigner/iStock/Getty Images Plus; DeAgostini/G. SIOEN; Daniel Osterkamp/Moment; halecr/E+; Arctic-Images/Corbis Documentary; Tammy616/iStock/Getty Images Plus; Nasser Mar/EyeEm; Antonello/Moment Open; Matteo Colombo/DigitalVision; Roberto Machado Noa/LightRocket; Justin Sullivan/Getty Images News; xavierarnau/E+; DEA/W. BUSS/De Agostin; Lintao Zhang/Getty Images Entertainment; Victor Moriyama/Getty Images News; Photography taken by Mario Gutiérrez./Moment; Medioimages/Photodisc; U6: denozy/iStock/Getty Images Plus; AJ_Watt/E+; Geber86/E+; Sam Edwards/OJO Images; skynesher/E+; Rob Daly/OJO Images; Terry Vine/Blend Images; Education Images/Universal Images Group; Blue Jean Images; PeopleImages/E+; LeoPatrizi/E+; Warren Photography/Warren Photography; JGI/Jamie Grill/Blend Images; kali9/iStock/Getty Images Plus; Westend61; Oleh_Slobodeniuk/E+; filadendron/E+; blackred/E+; Westend61; alikemalkarasu/E+; xxmmxx/E+; Wavebreakmedia/iStock/Getty Images Plus; Klaus Vedfelt/Riser; Erik Isakson/Blend Images; U7: sanjeri/E+; VCG/Contributor/Visual China Group; Kevin Dodge/Corbis; Jamie Grill; Lorado/E+; Lumina Images/Blend Images; powerofforever/E+; Tribalium/iStock; Hill Creek Pictures/UpperCut Images; Steve Debenport/E+; Cate Gillon/Staff/Getty Images News; ivanastar/iStock/Getty Images Plus; MatiasEnElMundo/iStock/Getty Images Plus; Deepak Sethi/iStock/Getty Images Plus; MangoStar_Studio/iStock/Getty Images Plus; Westend61; Jose Luis Pelaez Inc/Blend Images; U8: Erik Von Weber; Coldimages/iStock/Getty Images Plus; grafvision/iStock/Getty Images Plus; catalby/iStock/Getty Images Plus; Michel Tripepi/EyeEm; drnadig/E+; Krakozawr/E+; Grace Cary/Moment; baona/iStock/Getty Images Plus; Michael Burrell iStock/Getty Images Plus; kasto80/iStock/Getty Images Plus; Wavebreak Media/Getty Images